THE SURVIVOR'S PATH

Cover photograph by Victor Pavon.

Otto Grünfeld was born in Prague in 1924. Before the Second World War his family lived in the Sudeten, where his father was involved in business, as well as in the capital. He was attending grammar school in Prague when the Germans invaded in 1939.

Throughout, his interests have centred on music and psychology, the former being the basis to his professional life as a teacher, the latter a springboard to the craft of counselling. He is married and the father of five children, now all grown up. He has lived for the last forty years in North Yorkshire in England.

THE SURVIVOR'S PATH

THE STORY OF MY WAR

BY
OTTO GRÜNFELD

AISLABY
1995

© Otto Grünfeld

First published in Prague 1995
Second edition published by
Sessions of York 2001

ISBN 1 85072 271 4

Printed in 11½ on 14 point Plantin
by Sessions of York
The Ebor Press
York, England

Contents

	Page
Preface	vii
Jew	1
Prague	7
Terezín	17
Auschwitz	30
Kaufering	41
Allach	67
Prague	75
London	86
Postscript	97

I have written the following account of my experiences for my family, especially for my children, who do not doubt me but wish to know more of what really happened; also for myself with the desire to act as witness to events inspired and persecuted by evil, to which man is free to surrender and pay allegiance, and does so when he allows his mind to be polluted and his conscience to be anaesthetised.

Acknowledgements

If it had not been for William McEnchroe, the first publication of this book would never have been realised. This second edition is largely due to the interest and support of Sessions of York.

Preface

WHEN HE CAME to speak to me my mind was still with the voice of my wife speaking from England. I had telephoned Rosemary from the States – from a superstore in Milwaukee, to be precise.

'I heard you speak with a foreign accent. Excuse me, I hope you don't mind me asking you where you live?' I was certainly quite unprepared for that kind of questioning from a stranger. He looked like a mature student, with a strong-featured sallow face like someone from the Mediterranean.

'Yes, I live in England', I said naively, thinking he spotted an English accent. He knew better, though. 'Are you English, then?'

'No, British', but then, I wonder why, I added – 'I come from Czechoslovakia.'

'That's interesting. Were you a soldier in the last war?'

'No, actually I was interned', I heard myself say, beginning to feel a little uneasy. Are all Americans so curious? I had not noticed so far.

'Interned ?'

'Well, yes, I was in a Nazi concentration camp for being a Jew.'

'Really. And where were you interned, then?' There was an edge to his voice.

I told him. And this was his reply:

'That's a lot of Zionist propaganda. There was no such thing as a holocaust and concentration camps and all that', and he looked at me with scorn.

What I should have done was to walk away or, better still perhaps (but I am not at all sure, for brain-washing is easily achieved, eagerly accepted when it is expedient, truth becoming quite irrelevant), better perhaps hit him.

I am not in that line and, instead, I began to argue, but became terribly angry within, with a strange sense of desperation, of hopelessness, futility, a sense of a solemn and sacred cause besmirched, despoiled. My response was fierce but short-lived and fairly incoherent, and then I walked away quickly, quite shattered. I had experienced Satanic play in broad daylight and I felt the filth and evil palpably, an assault on reason and conscience. And I have been haunted by it ever since.

Jew

MY FAMILY BACKGROUND is fairly ordinary, I believe. My father left an impoverished farm in Slovakia and made his way to Vienna to undertake business studies, and from there to Náchod in North-East Bohemia where he met my mother. They worked in the same factory as junior clerks, my mother employed as a shorthand typist. They were engaged for eight years before getting married, and then moved home several times, whenever father found a more desirable and demanding post elsewhere. He travelled extensively to promote his firm's business, at the same time climbing steadily on the ladder to success as a result of his dedication and business acumen.

My brother and I were brought up in an uneventful middle-class milieu basically no different from any other white collar worker. Our life-style was unostentatious, almost modest, our expectations circumscribed by my father's insistence that the inevitable gap between worker and clerk in terms of status and income be kept within certain limits. Bless him for this thinking and for acting on such principles when he was made an executive, although it did not help him – or us – one little bit in the years to come.

In religious terms 'Jewishness' had all but died in our family, even if the occasional visit to my grandparents in Náchod prompted a brief and somewhat trying revival of orthodoxy, displaying itself in all the minutiae of Sabbath observance, prayers at night said in Hebrew repeated word by word after grandma (but not understood), kosher cuisine, and the inevitable attendance in grandfather's synagogue when he would lead the chanting and singing with his gorgeous lyric tenor voice. The boredom for us children was almost insufferable as nothing but the occasion itself made it real for us.

As for grandmother's fierce observance of kosher principles, noteworthy of mention were two large sideboards equipped with almost identical crockery and cutlery, but strictly separate in function, since one was used exclusively for milky, the other for meaty food. It kept us spellbound until suddenly shocked by grandma's furious remonstrations when she found a 'milky' spoon in amongst the 'meaty' ones in the drawer.

After a visit to Náchod, however, we were relieved to resume our habitual freedom, feeling liberated. And that, I assume, was our designated religious status, being liberal Jews. It meant no rituals, no observances, no kosher food for us, merely a religious acknowledgement during the Passover and the Day of Atonement (Yom Kippur) festivals, curiously less significant to us than Christmas.

Had the Jewish religion, let alone orthodoxy, lost its hold on our family? My aunt Edith, my mother's sister, told me once after the war was over, with a mischievous grin, how our cantor grandfather – a cantor representing the liturgical leader of a congregation, second only to the rabbi – had occasionally and secretly indulged in eating the odd pork sausage, horror of horrors to an orthodox Jew. If she knew, then so did her three sisters and brother. A tiny door had been opened to allow liberalism to enter by means of ritualistic treachery by one who was a highly respected member of the local Jewish community and, moreover, a most kind-hearted and generous philanthropist.

• • •

'Jew!'

'Jew!'

'Jew!'

The yells came from my school-fellows out on the street as I sped home from school, all of six years old, barely 'hatched', uncomprehending, my heart beating fast, my soul in anguish. This was a hard blow to my confidence in the world out there which, a moment before, I had felt so safe in.

Obviously I had not taken in the implications following the formal questioning of each child by the teacher on the first day of each new school year. 'Name?' 'Date of birth?' 'Religion?'

It dawned on me later that my German sounding name did not endear me to my Czech class mates. Deeper layers of aversion were stirred up when, red in the face and desperately self-conscious, having offered my tell-tale name, I had to add the fatal word 'Jewish'. What I began dimly to sense in my early school years became a certainty in my teens, the fact that my standing in class and among some teachers was irredeemably flawed, my chances of progress in terms of personal growth and learning clearly prejudiced.

School, this apparently inflexible world I was exposed to, away from the protective cloak of home, presented from the onset an inscrutable and untrustworthy face, making me wary and withdrawn, watchful and defensive as the years passed. I stayed behind my barrier when the word 'Jew' was spoken among the children in class, and I pretended not to have heard, although anger and frustration rose within me and my whole being smarted. Spoken to my face was another matter. I was forced, by some inner logic, to retaliate by battling it out, but, like so many children's fights, the original cause was forgotten after the first heat of the encounter, and the former status quo was resumed. In my case that meant stepping back behind my barrier again and hoping, if not really believing, that the conflict had brought about a resolution.

Some teachers played the game more subtly, such as withholding praise, by indifference, by remarks on the borderline of ridicule, though calculated to be noticed by the class.

'Grünfeld, you are a piece of wood, and not a rare kind, either', says my physics master.

'Bluefeld, are you paying attention?' says another. 'Blackfeld, were you sleeping?'

Eventually, Jewish children were barred from attending state schools altogether, so that, at the age of sixteen, I entered a Jewish school. My relief was profound, in the fullest sense of the word. My results in class rose dramatically and I became a contented and involved student, an experience entirely novel to me.

My 'phoney war' was not only waged at school, of course, but was fought out of school whenever I had to face situations beyond the sphere of my home. These battles occurred on a more subtle plain. Where my school-mates had sometimes become crudely abusive, grown-ups disposed of a more hidden means to hurt me, embarrass me and marginalise me.

'I never knew you were a Jew. You are so different.'

That did not help. In fact it cemented the barriers already there, although, for a moment, I found myself on the wrong side of the divide, exposed, on trial. Having succumbed to flattery, I would emerge instantly with a sense of deep guilt, as though I had betrayed my side. An inner conflict was afoot, a kind of double-bind, leading to the conundrum – to be a Jew or not to be a Jew. But having been lured across the barrier of my own making made me, in a curious way, more conscious of being a Jew.

All of this was kept hidden, not a word breathed to my parents, nor shared with my brother. So far the phoney war had been a private affair.

• • •

Before the German troops entered the country in 1938, even before the short spell of the Protectorate era, my father had to relinquish his position as head executive of the textile firm Hernych and Son in the little town of Ustí nad Orlicí, where we lived. To a man of my father's ambition this must have been a terrible blow, as it must have been for my mother who, I know, liked to bask in the limelight of my father's position. There was no other option, nor any prospect of another one; the gates had shut and father had to make the best of things, working in many devious ways through his ubiquitous business connections to eke out a viable living. I did not realise the enormity of what had happened to him, and to all of us for that matter; the clear message slipped away, adding to the store of accumulating wrongs.

Yet this was no longer my own private and secret affair, as there was no hiding the fact that we had to pack our things and move from a comfortable large home and gardens into a small flat in Prague, in the process disposing of the larger part of our antiques and many other items, including our cherished bikes! We also gave shelter to my father's sister-in-law, my aunt Rosa, who had been forced to leave Vienna, with all her hopes focused on joining her refugee daughter working as a domestic in London, hopes which were to die with her in a concentration camp. This move, the first of three such moves into increasingly cramped accommodation before the final fiasco of the break-up of the family, saw us gradually become more strongly and deeply united, the external pressures acting like flux. And, at the same time, a widening crack appeared in what had till recently felt like an invincible protective armour of family security, initially induced by the loss of father's position and our first move, and now followed by others, as blow fell upon blow.

Prague

1941

I SEE US WALKING down a street in Prague, carrying a very large and heavy parcel: our beautiful and almost new big radio, as well as two old guns (how we had loved playing with them, especially the big Colt!) and my father's Browning revolvers, one of which he used to take on his travels. My older brother Paul and I manhandled our burden with a heavy heart, our sense of justice injured, our feelings troubled; a distinctly uneasy foreboding was in peculiar contrast to the ordinariness of our surroundings: the passing traffic on the street, people walking along the pavements casting the occasional casual glance in our direction.

There were a number of places of collection where Jews had to deliver items not allowed to be in their possession any longer. This was one instance which impinged strongly on my innocent mind because, despite former petty but unpleasant persecutions by some of my school-fellows, this hit below the belt, turning the occasional victimisation, or heat of sudden boyish conflict, into a gnawing existential fear deep down in my being. These domestic possessions we were surrendering were symbols of privacy and freedom, which gradually and irresistibly were to be curtailed and eventually eliminated.

The nationwide census of all Jews was another and deeper blow, earmarking each one of us as a potential target. Apart from the brave few who managed to slip out of the official net we submitted in almost total resignation.

The personal affront peaked with the introduction of the Jewish Star, that ugly piece of yellow cloth with the word JUDE inscribed in the centre, to be worn visibly on all occasions on our outer garments; the sternest punishment was threatened for disobeyance. Thus marked and singled out we became public targets of the official Nazi doctrine of Jewish inferiority, driven into the realm of 'righteous' contempt by the Herrenfolk who could deal with us as they pleased. The humiliation was, it seemed to us, completed, so much so that I, at any rate, almost believed it would and could not go any further.

How fateful that my bid for freedom had been thwarted. For just before these events took place my emigration as a Zionist, to go to Israel, appeared to have been finalised. Two bulky suitcases were already waiting at the railway station, the transport to go within a few days, as others had gone before. But mine was the first to be stopped and I remember carting the heavy pieces back home with the utmost difficulty, yet with relief. The project had been fraught with doubt, anyway: digging the virgin soil of Palestine (as it was then called) and playing the piano were incompatible activities. As Zionists we all knew that hard manual work was a 'must' to get the country on the road to viable nationhood, and my conflict was between idealism and self interest, the former blossoming when among my peers, the latter when by myself. I was glad therefore to return home and, unpacking my music before all else, I rushed to my piano to claim back my personal life. I am glad now, in retrospect, exceedingly glad, not to have gone away; I would have felt a traitor to my family going into comparative safety, away from the catastrophic events which overtook Europe, and us Jews in particular.

So much has been said about the origins of Jewish persecution that it would be foolish of me here to attempt an explanation. However, I can speak with justification of its effects. Being on the receiving end a peculiar logic of its own begins to operate in a victim's mentality which has little to do with reasoning, but a lot with a covert, often sly, opportunism. I would hate to think that people believed I had been heroic. Far from it. Expediency was a capital virtue, the tool for survival, and I used it whenever a chance presented itself. To my shame I will admit now how good it felt not having to wear the Jewish Star right from the beginning, not until some time later, since my domicile was in Slovakia and Slovak Jews had a certain protection for a limited period. So, for a while, I felt privileged.

We Jews still managed to make distinctions between ourselves, a stupid, petty and quite sickening attitude: the Austrian Jew disliked the Russian Jew, the German Jew the Austrian Jew, the Czech the German Jew. It never reached the level of hatred and, under common threat, we instinctively felt as one. But we continued to make these distinctions, right through the terrible events which were to overtake us.

• • •

It was late Spring in 1942.

This is the time when my war began and I want to share some of it with you especially, Paul.

Had it not been that father tried to get us out of the country – too late, as it happened, although he had been warned and good friends had begged him to take the whole family abroad sooner, since he had so many good connections – and, in the process, fallen into a trap set by the Gestapo in order to fill their own pockets, you and I would not have been thrown together the way we were. Instead, we would have gone to Terezín as a family.

Well I remember a Jewish lady friend bursting into our flat one day with the news that rich friends of hers had been released from one of the transports, now in full swing, and had returned home. She was in a state of frenzy almost, as though such a reversal of fate was apocalyptic. The excitement which took hold of us was unbelievable, although cool reason would have demanded caution. However, as the credentials seemed impeccable contact was made with a certain German 'civilian' (with the highest connections, we were told) whose assumed name was Melke. I became the courier for the delivery of the required goods, the payment for our safety: gold, diamonds, valuables, currency. I can even recall delivering American dollars my father had managed to conjure up.

Then we were called in, all of us, to join the transport, wondering whether the miracle would happen. And then the news came, a few hours later: 'You can take your things and go home. There has been a mistake.'

How can I describe our elation, how, again, I felt different from other people, privileged, chosen. We had won!

A few weeks later the blow fell.

I do not believe I ever told you what it was like when the Gestapo crashed their way into the flat very early one morning, ordered us to get dressed, and hustled us out into the street and the waiting cars. You were out, remember, doing your own thing as usual, some physical training or whatever. They were not bothered, they just took who was there: father, mother, our aunt Rosa, and me. The drive to the Petschek Palais, the Gestapo Headquarters in Prague, was terrible. To see my father, always held up as, and felt to be, the personification of invincibility, manhandled and disposed of like anyone else, made my old world split apart and vanish forever. Through the empty streets we drove, straight to the notorious place of horror, the place of interrogation and torture, and taken into the large waiting room filled with people sitting in rows like in a school room, despondent and frightened, in expectation of the typical sadistic questioning. An armed guard walked up and down alongside the walls.

I do not believe I told you how father turned round trying to make eye contact, intending some communication in the throbbing stillness of this anteroom of hell; how the guard became alerted, started to shout, and as father was taken out I had to perform endless knee bends. I kept going on mechanically – it did not seem to matter. Then I was made to sit again and I stayed on in that place for two, perhaps three hours, how can I tell? Then they sent me home. I did not share with you what went on there, or inside me, the sheer panic and dread and incomprehension of it all; yet, this crazy acceptance of it, as if a decree of God Himself had been in operation.

How strange to walk back to our flat unable to accommodate or reject this experience, just like so many other experiences which were to follow.

What did it feel like for you, Paul, when you eventually came home to see me wide-eyed, terrified, realising that father, mother and aunt were gone, to return when? in what state? ever? You understood so much more clearly than I could what was at stake, for you were informed, older, much more aware. The ghastly truth must have dawned on you, and you had the added burden of keeping the full weight of truth from me; you had a child on your hands to protect, no doubt.

• • •

They were gone, leaving the remnants of our former secure familiarity and domesticity in our bewildered hands. We lived with one persistent and unspoken hope: that they would be released and come back home again. Hope, hope ... hope was my plaything, but engulfed by heavy presentiments.

Really, I was not of much help to you running the home for us, was I, Paul? It was all a bit chaotic, and I must have been under some shock, slowed down and lethargic. You went out and worked hard for long hours and, I am sure, were expecting, when you got home, some welcome and a nice meal. All you found was me, probably not much of a welcome, and an indifferent fare scrambled together in my novitiate's ignorance of cooking. I never told you that I found it too hard to cope with it all, with our dear ones now in prison, transports departing one after another, and all these duties to keep us two going. To think was also to feel, to feel was to fear, a fear which, as time went on, became an ever more undermining companion, always there, behind, beneath, within: did you not find it so, too? But, of course, we never mentioned fear; we never mentioned mum or dad except when it was time to get the little suitcase with a fresh change of clothing ready to take to the prison, and pass it through the tiny window to a guard with an expressionless face.

Remember that little handkerchief with a heart embroidered in one of the corners, 'greetings meadow green' inscribed inside it in Czech: mum's last message to us? I still have it, believe it or not. Aunt Edith found it in the flat after we had left for Terezín. It took years for me to translate the message into meaning; it says: 'Your mother loves you.' What took me thirty years or more I am sure you understood straight away and quietly filed it away. I seem to have been trailing life by so many years. I care not to count.

This must have been a drag to you, and sometimes you became impatient with me when, after a day's work, you came home to find that the few jobs you had asked me to do, especially those connected with our impending internment, had been 'forgotten.' The meal was there at least, but that was done only after I had immersed myself in my piano playing, these ceaseless and largely abortive battles with technique absorbing my attention and my energy, a useful if frustrating smokescreen put between myself and the cruel world out there.

You understood? After all you had studied psychology, you were going to be a doctor, you would have known something about defences we build for self-protection. In a way I suppose it was a relief for both of us when we were called up into the next transport – it was June – and subsequently were identified as BD20 and BD21, sucked into the voracious machine of deportation. No more shopping or cooking or washing for me, with that feeling of inadequacy, knowing that my efforts would inevitably fall below the standards the two of us had taken for granted all our life.

But I cannot remember you ever criticising this part of my duties, Paul; nor did we share any of our feelings or thoughts on all the things which oppressed our minds.

Despite that I can see now how lucky we were at least to have each other, how lucky I was to have you there by my side, always competent, always so together ... or am I wrong? Were your own doubts and fears gnawing inside you just as much as they were within me?

At this time we were raided by the Czech police one night, an incident I shall never forget or forgive, causing a deep shock to my juvenile belief in the Czech cause. The big fellows ransacked the flat and carried away anything they fancied, eventually leaving us standing among the debris of our belongings, uncomprehending. It felt like a stab in the back after they had left, giving us a further warning about the perfidy men in uniform so often embrace.

Anyway, to get the two big suitcases ready was no problem. Strange, I do not remember walking out of the flat, out of the house, to go to the Exhibition Complex, the assembly place for all the transports. It helped, I suppose, that we had had to move three times recently on account of restrictions imposed on Jews becoming ever more stringent. Each move helped to loosen our identification with a home, helped to make us more effective pilgrims. And, frankly, any searching thoughts on what was really happening were out of the question. Questions were not asked.

We simply had to get on with it, as best we knew.

Supposing I was forced to walk out of my home as a result of an order, to be press-ganged into deportation under some stupid pretext, carting me away to some unknown destination for an indefinite period of time (forever?) to do I know not what, together with strangers thrown together somehow, to live a life beyond imagining: surely I would do so with a despairing heart, in revulsion and opposition to such incredible monstrosity, such madness. Having my life shattered for being a Jew could not possibly reconcile me to such a fate.

But no, I had no such struggle. I did not even look back as we left the house, my mind already on what promised to be an exciting expedition, an opportunity to shed my oppressive responsibilities and start afresh. My only worry was: had we forgotten something important we could not do without? And would our parents eventually join us? It was this hope that kept up my spirit, the hope of reunion obliterating what would otherwise have felt like a final tearing out of my very roots.

We walked into the old-fashioned wooden Exhibition Centre, loaded under the weight of our cases, and picked out our sleeping places on the floor of the primitive empty hall. I think we were given palliasses. We met a few people we knew.

I wonder, Paul, how you felt about this, to what extent you protected me by what you said or omitted to say, what your apprehensions were? What were your hopes of father and mother rejoining us? I wish I knew. You see, I have no measure to gauge your stature, no means to reach your vulnerability. It is always I who comes to the forefront and fills the scenario. I know it was I who relied on you; but who was your support?

The Exhibition Centre began to fill over a period of days during which we managed to keep ourselves entertained by playing games and rushing about, for there were no guards to keep us in check. Newcomers of all ages, men, women and children, arrived at intervals, exhausted and apprehensive, laden with baggage. We were asked to help carry their stuff to their sleeping places and I remember joining with such wild enthusiasm and energy, picking up all the heaviest burdens and running back for more, that I suddenly collapsed, hardly realising I had seriously overtaxed my strength.

And sure enough, when we were eventually marched to the railway station very early one morning, my baggage seemed to weigh tons and kept slipping out of my grasp. I felt odd.

Then the train journey and yet another march – a long one this time – from the station to the fortress Terezín, a march proving a great ordeal for me as my physical condition was no longer equal to it.

But at last, in through the gates, into the Ghetto, my home to be.

Terezín

TEREZÍN WAS NOT just a prison: it was, and still is, a sizeable fortress town built by order of the Empress Maria Theresa at the end of the eighteenth century. In her days it must have seemed an immense and invincible fortification which could withstand months and years of siege, a strategic miracle then, but rendered obsolete in the course of time and improved methods of human destructiveness.

For you, Paul, and for me, it was a march into a world undreamed of, a march into a strange new life full of hidden challenges and demands. Basically a garrison town with a square in the middle, a church, numerous large barracks built in quadrangles, and small dwellings no doubt built to house the large numbers of camp followers who were part of an army's contingent, it was in appearance unattractive, a purely functional establishment. As we were to find out it was then entirely run by Jewish administration under direct orders from the German Commandant and his staff, housed in the 'Kommandantur', their headquarters, in the centre of the town. You know how we were separated almost immediately and I was assigned sleeping quarters in some barrack away from you. This seemed like a ghastly mistake to me, made worse by my temporary physical weakness and dependency.

I felt forsaken, but I do not think you realised that, Paul, when you came to see me and tried to make me pluck up courage. I felt exhausted and quite desolate.

The following day I was assigned to work in a team of male newcomers ordered to dig out a tree! I felt completely useless, staggering under the weight of my pick axe; even to shovel seemed beyond my strength, and I could not understand what was going on till, eventually, I blurted out desperately that I just could not manage. The leader of the team then decided to give me permission to return to barracks. In Terezín that was possible, in the concentration camps such a move would have had fatal consequences.

Paul, I was so very envious of your good fortune to get together with your Zionist cell members and occupy a special room – a kitchen with an iron kitchen stove – in the large barrack made into a children's home next to the church, right on the large square. When I came to realise the full implications of my separation from you my yearning to join you reached unendurable proportions. Was it you, or your friends, or was it my urging, which smoothed the path towards getting us together? I am not at all sure. What mattered was that I was allowed to move in with you at last, although it felt to be a temporary favour, into this haven of a kitchen cum bedroom cum living room, with the status of a junior guest tolerated, if not exactly welcomed.

Apart from you and Sigi there were Joschka and Manci, Egon and Bertik, Pét'a and Jenda. I had forgotten most of these names, but they come back to me as I write, a resurrection of memory I find exciting. We did form a community by way of sharing the food including some parcels sent by dear aunt Edith), sharing ideas, arguing, and niggling, of course. For me it was a great opportunity to form an identity through entering this fairly gentle melée of older boys. Also, I felt almost secure, almost cosy, relaxed, and gradually this togetherness became the haven I needed, especially as I was not well, could not work like all the others, yet was given space to rest and hang around.

There is the memory of trying to walk up a staircase with the greatest effort, like an old man, and I am sure I had either strained my heart or suffered from shock. But after some time the boys began to grumble and believed I was dodging work. How very embarrassing it must have been for you, Paul. Dodging was considered to be unacceptable since work meant extras in food allocation and aided opportunities to 'organise' edibles to augment our limited diet. Joschka the baker brought additional 2kg loaves of bread after most shifts; Manci the gardener fruit and vegetables; Pét'a potatoes; Egon the cook, who also served at one of the numerous hatches where the food for the day was being distributed for the 40,000 or so inmates, would, when he saw one of us, keep on ladling into our communal bucket long after the prescribed amount was reached.

'Schmeh' was the word generally used by us when we engaged in deceit, pilfering, daylight 'robbery' of communal property. We had little conscience over such matters, and since no questions were asked none needed to be answered. A kind of free-for-all without violence or bloodletting, 'civilised' crime indulged in by all (except the truly principled) who found the opportunity, a communal maladjustment not uncommon elsewhere.

All of this I learned by and by. As I was rolling about in our quarters and began to look around town, still with nothing to do, the news came one day which crushed my spirit and laid me totally prostrate: news of the death of my father and mother in Mauthhausen and Auschwitz. The anguish which then overpowered me, a physical as well as mental pain, was so intense that for days I lay on my bed weeping, sobbing, grieving. A deep and hidden dread had surfaced into a reality I was unable to cope with so that, after a prolonged period of sorrowing, I sank into hopelessness and depression.

Paul, you could not help me except by your nearness and my assumption about your own grief. I do not think we talked or consoled each other .You must have struggled hard to absorb this shock and carry on your life, more so as I was a burden among you. You could not give me gentle consolation, cradle me in your arms to hold my broken self together. You did your coping well, I am sure, but I saw none of it, for I had moved myself away, I crawled into some dark solitary corner of my being, struggling in a vain battle. How long did all this take? When was it that I began to open my eyes to look around, cautiously to take in the world around me? I just do not know. I heard the odd remark then, sensed the growing impatience of my friends which won over their initial concern for me. Was it days, or weeks?

Gradually, however, energy began to seep back into me, a restlessness, even curiosity, about what was going on around me. I began to visualise getting out and about starting work, joining everyday life. What had seemed an unimaginably difficult task gradually appeared more acceptable, and so, with a push or two and a bit of wheeling and dealing I was persuaded to start work as a baker on eight hour shift work, like Joschka. Surely this came as a great relief to you, Paul. It meant this young brother of yours ceased to be a nuisance and a liability, a lazy and depressed layabout. I am sure it meant the end of a humiliation you could have done without during your own period of grief.

Oddly enough the full consequences of my parents' death did not become apparent as they would have done under normal circumstances. In this limbo existence of the Ghetto, where all normal contacts had been broken, all continuity disrupted, any future opportunity barred, their death also came out of context, a fantastic and unbelievable caricature of reality. Despite the unusual privilege of being informed of where they had died and when, we ourselves were castaways as they had been, but distanced from each other, fatefully beyond reach of each other. Where normally the family would unite in honouring and grieving together, burying their dear ones in joint mutual support, here we were simply left grappling with our sorrow until we were able to extricate ourselves from this incredible trauma and stagger on, somehow. Without the norm, custom, ritual, or close support which would help to grasp the inevitable truth and thus help us on the way there emerged, strangely, a sense of unreality sometimes strong enough to awaken deep down within me a vague sense that the news had been false. This condition I was to experience again later on.

During the tiring hours at work in the bakery, especially during the night shifts, I would try to sound out colleagues of my father's age to find if they had known him, and if so, under what circumstances, searching for a trace, a connection, some familiar – however little – part of him who belonged to me and who had been banished from me. You see, Paul, you could not be my brother properly just then because of your own deep problems, even less could you become a substitute father figure. My whole being longed hungrily for a reunion of some kind, and I went on looking even for the smallest crumbs to give me some comfort. I looked in vain, but carried on looking all the same for years, even now.

'Did you say his name was Morris? Don't think I knew him,' said one, when asked.

'Hernych and Sons, the textile works. Yes I know the firm. Don't remember a Grünfeld,' said another, and started talking about relatives in the States he was going to join after the war.

Once a colleague said: 'Sure I remember the name, but can't think in which connection. Did you say textile? You lived in Ustí? Ustí nad Labem?' We had lived in Ustí nad Orlicí when father worked for Hernych and Son. I drew yet another blank. Of course I did not tell you about all that, Paul. I was much too shy and, anyway, you might have thought I was being silly.

Inevitably, regular hard work, even under bad conditions, made me grow stronger and better adjusted, even if, to start with, I barely managed to survive the long dreary hours. Built within the ramparts of the fortress the bakery was a rambling succession of long and low vaulted halls accommodating the flour processing shop, mixing room with two or three mixing machines, a loaf processor, and the main baking hall with two large old-fashioned coal-fired baking ovens and one modern steam oven. We baked about 80 to 90 2kg loaves a time in each oven right through the consecutive shifts, producing thousands of loaves per day. I do not remember that you ever entered the premises, Paul. As far as I was concerned I could not get out fast enough at the end of the stuffy-aired and smoke-filled shift, hiding two or even three of those big loaves inside my clothing, and slinking fearfully past the Jewish guardsmen – unarmed – stationed at the large gates. It must have been obvious what we all did, but the guards were unconcerned and unseeing. Of course there was pride in bringing freshly baked loaves to help in feeding us, or be used as currency, as well as the pay-off in the form of a measure of admiration for my thieving skills.

• • •

It was perhaps an irony of fate which enabled me to make a discovery which influenced my life in Terezín, and later after the war, in quite a profound way. Idly strolling one day into the inner quadrant of the Magdeburg barracks I noticed some very large crates standing in one corner. I had never been in this particular building, nor can I possibly imagine what made me go in that day. I cannot even guess what drew me to go near one of those crates and move a damaged board to see what was inside. To my utter amazement it was a black and almost new upright piano. And some deeper urge still made me prize open another board to expose the upper rear part of the instrument. There it was, unmistakable: O.G., my piano! I had scratched the initials on the back soon after my parents bought it for me, needless to say without their knowledge.

The excitement was immense. A bit of my home had come into the Ghetto. A bit of my life which I could be reunited with. I rushed into the nearest office and by degrees found the person responsible for musical instruments.

'Yes, maybe it's yours. No, sorry, you can't have it, of course, but we will allow you to practice on our pianos.' Bureaucracy delayed awhile but, eventually, I not only received a practice schedule, I even found a first-rate teacher, Bernhard Kaff, to give me weekly lessons in exchange for a quarter loaf of bread and the commitment to make his bed every second day. A hopeful new era began.

There came a time when I felt safe enough to enter more deeply into our community life. There again, Paul, I acted without your knowledge, developing my own way to draw closer to each member and make him speak about himself. I suppose they did not tell you about it; they might have been somewhat embarrassed perhaps. But for me these quiet sessions, when the room was empty except for the two of us, became a way to a better understanding of your friends through getting to know more about their background and what they stood for. For all I know they might even have enjoyed it, or been slightly taken aback by my concentrated focus on themselves. I know it was not mere curiosity, rather making up lost time, accommodating myself to our apparently more settled situation.

Why did Bertík – the comic, the one full of humour and fun, with the disposition of a happy child – why did he have to leave us before his time, aged nineteen? I think I loved Bertík more than any of my communal friends; perhaps because of his guileless innocence, his easy manner, his utterly unthreatening mode of being. Oh why did he have to go from us? Of course he would not have survived the incredible rigours and deprivations which lay in store for us in a few months time. He was, like most of us, a rather pampered Jewish boy, slim, quite delicate; and Terezín was, in some respects, a mild form of internment.

The dysentery which started his slow but unstoppable decline seemed, to begin with, just a minor nuisance, alleviated by our presence and his unfailing ability to crack a joke and grin. I see his grin even now, his round face and his horn-rimmed glasses. But his humour began to fade, his cheeks fall in, his eyes to look larger, sadder and more anxious, his body became skeletal. He was transferred to the infirmary, a cheerful and respectable place in the same building, and we visited a few times. There seemed to be no means to save him, however, and the shock of his death felt like a bad omen, a strange dull premonition. I do not believe funerals were permitted; I do not remember a service held for him, nor a send-off, or prayer, and I do not recall his parents being present. An unnecessary death? Who knows? But it was a deep, deep loss to us all of a special and beloved person.

It is strange how little I was aware, at the time, of the general situation and organisation of the Terezín Ghetto. How did the people live, work, manage their lives, cope with their problems, and how could they effect changes within their restricted existence? I was indeed aware of the large contingent of German Jews whom we, as Czechs, looked upon with some disdain, often with misgiving, laying claim upon Terezín as a Czech domain! Such is the irony, or rather, to be blunt, such is the evil of oppression that it will foster fragmentation within the larger community. The way I and our small group were placed was fortunate inasmuch as Sigi, who was in charge of the children's home where we also lived, was a Czech running a home for German children. His involvement and our presence in their midst fostered a natural integration which in other circumstances would have had to be won by dint of opposition to a prevalent trend. Even so the good this achieved failed to operate beyond the confines of the home.

Protected as I was by the cosiness of our group, within the cheerful setting of the home with its constant bustle of lively and optimistic children, it is perhaps understandable, if not excusable, that I cared little for the gaining of uncomfortable insights into the seamy side of ghetto existence; for, although it was common knowledge among us, one which a casual walk through any quarter of the town would immediately confirm, I refused to turn any such knowledge into a deeper fellow feeling. Whereas the children were well looked after and the workers reasonably treated, even if not properly fed, the truly disadvantaged were the old people, both men and women, though the latter generally proved to be tougher. Physically they suffered because of inappropriate rations, but their chief problem was that the older they were the more prone they became to psychic traumatisation and a broken spirit. I imagine the death rate among them would have been disproportionately high.

We young ones hardly wanted to know. In our youthful arrogance we looked the other way. Had the German slogan 'Strength through Youth' found its way into our psyche, a perversion not noticed by us except in the occasional twinge of conscience swiftly brushed aside? Despite all that I could not help seeing the old folk obviously discarded, without function, eyes staring past me into some unattainably far and desirable distance, their thin shapes hidden in worn and oversized clothes, living in squalor in their crowded quarters, aimless, futureless and dispirited phantoms of a once prosperous past. And yet, I guess, our ignoring their plight and fast approaching death was an instinctive reaction in the fight for survival then just begun. Later, in the concentration camps, this technique was perfected to an astonishing degree, rendering our natures almost impregnable to such dangerous emotions as compassion, strictly reserved for our nearest and dearest.

. . .

When you started the building programme of constructing partitioned rooms in the vast lofts of the children's home, and worked on the high roofs to fix the dormer windows without any safeguard whatever, I lived through spasms of fear that you would tumble down to your death, Paul. The sight of you up there made me giddy and quite ill. I could not understand where and how you found the skills to do such work, and the more I admired you for what you did the more terrified I became that it would end in tragedy. But you appeared calm and collected as usual, ever my unsurpassable superior, but also my beloved brother, to whom I could turn in my need more than ever before.

Were you amused when I started going out with my first girlfriends (there were two who took an interest in me and who initiated our 'dates'), parading the streets in my free time in solemn converse or even in more solemn, and embarrassed, silence. Were you amazed at my stamina when, after an eight hour night shift, I went out to do some heavy digging on top of the ramparts for another six hours under Manci's management, just for bravado? Were you content at last to see me coping with my life without further setbacks? I so much hope you were, as the darkest clouds were gathering fast around us, and especially around you, about to turn to blackness and torturous death. These were the last good days left to you before Hell and Inferno took over.

I think I know why you got married at that time and I believe you did it for the wrong reasons. I remember talking to you but, of course, I could not change your mind. You felt obliged to vindicate a long and intimate friendship, particularly as the vague but ugly rumours about gas chambers were spreading through the Ghetto. And so Sigi took his Trude and you your M. as wives, and another room was found to accommodate the four of you, with the addition of myself. At first I thought I had lost you, but I was proved wrong. If anything our relationship deepened further, and I even felt – for the first time ever – that you needed me more than I needed you. For I was noticing a sadness in you I had never seen before, something I was unable to comprehend.

Now, what can I say? Speculate, make assumptions? In any case the Terezín days were drawing to a close, although we did not know it. My bug-ridden eyrie suspended high up against the end wall above your beds, for me an uncomfortable place in more than one sense, was not to serve me long. The eight of us plus three wives (Manci had been married before coming to the Ghetto) still congregated to share our meals, with me as cook of extras and server. But the couples did impinge upon the former unity with their heightened concern about their particular relationship and interests, and the two separate rooms symbolised a changed situation which to me did not feel to be an improvement.

• • •

It is only in retrospect that I realise the total cynicism and wickedness of the German regime to have decided to set up Terezín as an example of how they managed internment camps and as part of that propaganda to appease international opinion, to invite the Swedish Red Cross to make a visitation to see for themselves. Not only was this to brag about their supposed humanitarian methods, but, more importantly for them, to put a smoke-screen around the atrocities already being perpetrated in the numerous concentration camps scattered throughout Germany and elsewhere.

Your work, Paul, was but one miniscule part of a truly impressive exercise to put Terezín on the map as a decent, tolerant, well-supplied and well-organised large-scale institution. The whole town began to throb under the activities of refurbishing, restoring, decorating and otherwise upgrading all the parts of the town which the Red Cross staff would be directed to view. Materials never seen before became available in plentiful supplies, and no effort or labour was spared to change the image. It was well done, quite brilliant! We loved it, naturally, at first not knowing what it was all about, suspecting a possible change of policy towards us, perhaps even the possibility of an end to this crazy folly and a return to normal life.

The Red Cross Commission came and went, and, having created a brief but highly expectant respite, it was followed by a lull, a kind of holding of breath, a waiting for something more to happen. But gradually we allowed ourselves to admit to having been witnesses to a well-rehearsed show not intended for our benefit.

• • •

Autumn 1944. In October the major crisis exploded, heralding the mass transportations from Terezín to Auschwitz. The Jewish leadership was imprisoned, including a friend of my father and our protector so far, Dr Zucker and his young wife.

The Ghetto was in a state of near panic. The cattle trucks were lined up with German armed guards patrolling up and down, people herded in ... there was weeping and last embraces, families split, couples parted ... squeezing together I do not know how many into the trucks, a bucket in the middle – hurry, hurry – doors rolled shut with a thunder and padlocked. Then waiting and listening to shouts and commands outside, a heave and screech of braked wheels, and the slow but inexorable drag of a desperate human load into the outer darkness...

Auschwitz

MY RIVAL, MY better, you who always succeeded when I failed, won when I lost, you who had come first when I came last – you who were my supporter and consoler, the well-wisher who grew in warmth and understanding of my needy self, the last remaining stronghold in an incomprehensible threatening world – you and I had but three days left together, cramped among a mass of bodies in the cattle truck rolling on and on towards mass slaughter. Try as I may my mind refuses to reveal all the events of those long hours, even less so the feelings flooding over me, and which I had to battle against, for fear of being overwhelmed by fear! What was it like, one body among dozens of bodies thrown together almost in a heap? Yes, bodies, not persons or even people, nameless, faceless, spiritless, without will, defeated but for the occasional fierce outbursts of anger over an inch of space lost or claimed. Half a century has passed and what happened then defies clear remembrance; it must be lurking in some deep recess of my mind, I know it is there, but how heavily crusted over to defy full recognition?

Thus I proceed from vision to vision, some clearer than others, sometimes connected, sometimes not, but real to me for all that. And the need to recapture them drives me on to write even while it hurts.

As the weary hours passed on and on our human vestiges seemed to give way to lower animal needs and responses. This crowded togetherness resulted in a faint sense of being protected, despite the occasional nasty squabble. Our common growing hunger and thirst, under the same roof, gave us a kind of corporate identity, and the bucket in the middle of the truck for our relief a token to the only need which could not be denied. I do remember gloom, darkness, black night; the occasional voice emanating from someone somewhere – and falling silent; the rolling wheels, the clutter of the truck, the strange stillness when it stopped – sometimes for long periods, waiting for we knew not what; the discomfort growing in intensity as time passed, but, by far the worst, the growing fear deep down in the gut.

The condemned knows his fate. His growing fear of the approaching moment of execution is an inseparable enemy assailing the very entrails of his being. The soldier leaving his filthy trench to go into attack expects to be hit, as he has seen hundreds of his comrades around him hit, and killed, the enemy-fear within him as real as the fear without. But we had not been condemned as far as we knew, nor were we soldiers in action. We were merely a heap of disposable humanity caged and steam-rolled we knew not why, where to, or what for. With the condemned and the soldier we shared one thing in common, however: fear, fear, fear....We knew not of an axe to fall, a rope to strangle, a shot or shrapnel to fell us. There was but one reality: our mass of bodies in a rolling truck going some place we sensed was bad.

You were next to me. I felt your body next to mine, your presence, your will and strength to see this through – this thing – whatever it was. How much did you know, or guess? I am sure you knew more than I. You would have kept your eyes and ears open and taken in the rumours that had been circulating in Terezín and which I had refused to listen to, or think about. Did you realise a fateful hour was fast approaching, despite the slow rolling of the wheels beneath us? You even had the will to fight. Some insult or some aggression from some lout – no, another soul in anguish, but that I can only say now – provoked you into action within the most severe restriction of movement. Oh God, why did the blow aimed at you not shatter your glasses which you always wore? It might have saved your life.

And then, during the third night, we stopped, stood still for longer than ever. And we knew. How? Yes, we knew we had arrived, and the silence and the fear among us and within us became unbearable. Words fail.... What can I say but just say it and be done with...

I thought I had written about all this in my diary soon after coming to England, but I cannot find it now. I would have copied it here. Now I have waited for weeks since deciding to write about it, knowing I had to put it down on paper again in just so many words. I prevaricated. It feels almost obscene to describe in mere words what was paid for in life-blood; and how can I honour you, Paul, by putting down facts, with all this concern about my feelings, whilst yours, and your very self, were brutally extinguished, murdered? What did we say to each other? Was your mind as full of horror as mine was before the action began? But then, when our last hour came, it passed without a hand-clasp, without an embrace, without good-bye, without even a glance! What terrible parting, what breach, tearing away, a cracking break which stays there forever in its monstrosity and evil.

Dare I say this as well: a parting between us, however fleeting it were to have been, would have sealed my own fate as well. A memory of you leaving me, having parted thus, would have taken all my strength away, I know. What providence spared me then, and after, and to what purpose? The very barrenness and starkness of our final separation was unknown to both of us, a gift of life to me. For when I was to mourn you, my dearest brother, I could do so without seeing you as a loser; indeed, a vision of you going from me with a look of fear in your always brave eyes would have crushed me. This I am sure of.

Our train moved creakingly out of the dark into a lighted area visible through cracks and ventilation grids in the wagon, then ground to a halt. Immediately we were assailed by raucous shouts and commands of: 'Raus! Raus! Raus! Raus!' repeated over and over and over again along the whole length of the train, whilst the heavy doors of the trucks were unlocked and rolled open to reveal a platform alive with rough-looking men with armbands on their pyjama-like striped prison uniforms, as well as numbers of armed German guards. 'Raus! Raus!' screamed the voices, adding curses and insults, rifle butts hammering on the trucks. In the tumult our tension reached panic level; we scrambled out somehow, leaving our only and last belongings inside the foul-smelling vehicle.

The sight we met in this tumult was beyond grasp. We were a totally bewildered and terrified mass of 2,000 men, women and children, standing in a freezing night on a long platform lit by searchlights, surrounded by beastly alien creatures yelling, hitting, herding us into a queue. Some ghastly rectangular chimneys in the near distance were belching thick smoke with menacing flames making the sky glow an infernal crimson hue. A strange odour permeated the air and seemed to invade me with an indescribable horror.

My whole being screamed within as the yells out there surrounded me, screaming No! No! No! And the overwhelming flood of fear was incapable of release into an actual scream, or fight, or flight. Locked within my struggling self my impotence made me limp in defeat and humiliation, turning me into a trembling, dull, stupid and will-less creature. And standing there in that queue in the bitter cold I finally became a pawn in the grasp of most sinister powers.

Gradually we began to move forward to some point ahead of us. The incongruous sight of a table standing in the middle of the platform, with an impeccably dressed SS officer sitting behind it, met me unprepared.

'Name!'

'Age!'

'Occupation!'

You went first, as you always did, Paul.

My dear, my dear, you wore your glasses (oh, why had they not been smashed during your fight?), and you had dark brown hair, and brown eyes just like Mum, and that was enough. The racist creed of the man responded, a movement of the arm, a flick of the hand, a pointed finger, that was all that was needed. And you went...

My turn. Same questions. Paul, this I could not help; I looked more like dad: fair hair, blue eyes, no glasses. How was I to know? The arm moved, the finger pointed, and I went ahead following you. You must have known I was there, just behind you. The yell which issued, I dimly realised, was meant for me, and, turning, I saw the infuriated SS man directing me the other way. And I went.

This choice between us I never understood, not to this day, nor did I ever accept it. Part of me still wants to follow you where you went, but is too scared to do so. Another part of me lives in guilt that I should have been spared the ultimate horror of the gas chambers, the most bestial killing man ever undertook. I did try, later, to follow you where you had gone, but repeatedly failed, the mind boggling at the scenes it evoked. It was too frightening to enter the unspeakable you had been forced into. I just could not do it, Paul, I still cannot do it. And I feel guilty about that, too. Besides, I think that even if I could do it I would be killing you all over again, and this also I cannot bear. So the fears are locked within me, and the guilt, and the horror of what happened to you and all the innumerable others, as it had happened before to mum and dad and our aunt, compacting within me to form an impermeable core, a citadel, to withstand the forthcoming beleaguerment and constant assails. And when its defences were crumbling and shattering as the months, and later the years, went by, yet they were holding out, nevertheless, just holding.

And here I leave you, beloved, you who I know held me up through my great trials ... and does so still?

• • •

We were in Auschwitz. We had been sorted, the 'chaff' from the 'corn' (I saw myself as the former, always; the good corn was the victims sacrificed), those who appeared able from those who did not appear so, the women from the children, mothers from their babies except when they clung together and therefore were dispensed with as well.

Your way was the road to Calvary, Paul, but I, who went the 'other way', did not know it at the time, not till the following morning. Our remnant of a few hundred or was it a few dozen? – was marched to a large building, a kind of large shed, I think, where we were ordered to strip naked under the gaze of some SS men and some young uniformed women, laughing and joking between themselves, and processed through a shower and wash drill to the other end of the shed where we were thrown some old prison clothes. I saw traces of blood in the showers, I heard screams and shouts, it comes back to me now as I write. Did someone try to hide jewellery on his body? What happened?

Our possessions were fair game to those who were 'on duty', near to our shame and degradation, specimens of a human rapaciousness which knows no limit. As the great majority of the 2,000 strong transport had been exterminated and were being thrown into the fiery furnace as the night wore on, we who were left were bundled off wearing other victims' discarded clothing. We were herded into a compound surrounded by a high wire fence, and I remember a large wooden hut filled with sleeping prisoners clinging for life to their bit of space and snarling at us as we tried to find room to lay down our utterly exhausted and traumatised selves.

It was not sleep, it was not waking; it did not resemble anything I had ever experienced, and I cannot describe it. It must have been the culmination of the preceding hours, but without a consummation. The deepest layers of the unconscious must have taken over, guiding body and mind into an underworld of half-light, half-truth, half-reality, half-existence. A superb machinery of defences was in operation helping to minimise the unbearable, to dull the pain, limit realisation, exclude judgement, disregard values, dispense with choice. In my total powerlessness powers within took charge, undirected by myself, forcing me into violent, undreamed of adjustments and acceptances. I had become a human animal overnight, the night of my greatest darkness, but able to rise next morning to renewed shouts and commands ordering us out there to stand in the cold, feeling hungry and derelict.

Sometime during that first day we were given some soup which we ate standing around, for the hut was out of bounds for the day. And sometime during that day I received the blow that should have felled me, but did not. Hans Eisner was his name, a doctor from Hamburg, who had married my former and much beloved Hungarian piano teacher, Lizzy; they had a baby. I did not know they had been in the same transport as us, and now he suddenly materialised next to me, a crazed expression on his face. 'Where is Paul?' he said feverishly.

'I don't know,' I said.

'Why, were you not together?'

'He was told to go the other way on the platform,' I answered, sensing something awful as I looked at him.

'Paul is dead,' he almost screamed. 'Don't you know, can't you see the chimneys? They have gassed them!' They had gassed Lizzy and her baby, too, but I did not want to believe him. I had never liked the man. He had taken my beloved Lizzy from me whom I had owned in my heart for many years, he had seduced her and they had a baby, she had become a mother removed from me, our magic world of music had been broken by him, this stiff, abrupt, humourless man with clipped speech and an ugly Hamburg accent. I knew I had always hated him. He had also been a leader on a summer camp – quite the wrong person, much too old, anyway ...

There was no conversation between us. No comforting, no warmth whatsoever, just the sharp arrow which had missed the heart by a fraction, maybe because my heart was not available to him and I rejected his message as hard as I had rejected him. The ensuing battle within me was not allowed to reach any conclusion, my remaining strength being required elsewhere. I parried the blow by making myself believe Paul had escaped, that he had been picked out – being so able – to do something important, that he had gone to some other compound, etc. The more varied the possibilities of his survival, and however improbable, the more the force of the blow was diminished, thus saving energy to cope with the present.

I realised I was not quite on my own. Manci, Joschka and his brother were there, but, without Paul, I felt I had no claim on them, that I was just one among a large crowd and had no right to expect their friendship, thus discounting over two years' communal living. What today I know to have been a life-saving coincidence to have these friends beside me, forging close links between ourselves which helped us all, but especially me, to survive the gruesome months ahead, at that time I merely accepted this gift without surprise or joy, but as a given thing which I grasped and held on to, preoccupied as I was with coping, just coping. Events carried me like flood waters carry debris.

Our luggage was gone, our precious things – such as we might have had – stolen. Walking up and down in the compound from very early in the morning until dusk, with one bowl of soup to keep us going, we began to communicate with each other, exchanging information gathered from I know not whom, beginning to think ahead. For myself, and very likely for so many other bereaved, the time for talking had not yet begun. I was in shock, attempting to ward off despair by generating random hopes concerning Paul, then pushing all thought out of my mind. But then fear invaded me, followed by another onset of despair, and I commenced on another cycle of the same process.

Throughout the days which followed we were ordered several times to group into squads according to profession or skills. A choice was apparently being offered, some programme was in the offing, the first time in aeons. Somebody must have spread the word that declaring a profession – a sign of status and importance – might be dangerous and lead to disaster. My friends made the decision to stick together and opt for the lowest of all menial skills, i.e. labourer rather than teacher, clerk, etc., realising the German Nazi's hatred of the Jewish intellectual. This policy proved to have been the right one for us as it led to an early deportation from Auschwitz.

One vivid memory of importance comes to mind. As we were marching one night within the camp, passing a number of compounds, I saw several capos (prisoners with a function and some privileges, drawn from the ranks of the political prisoners, usually communists, as well as from the ranks of those convicted for criminal acts) standing on the side of the road. As we approached they started hitting those of us who marched on the edge of the column. I was one of those to receive a direct hit on the face, the first of only two I escaped with during my whole internment.

The shock was staggering, the memory of it never faded. The general law about guilt and punishment was obviously suspended in our situation, as I should have known, but the impact was aggravated by the fact that I had been singled out to be assaulted for the sole reason that I existed. I marched on, shaken to my roots, unable to either forget or forgive, my remaining balance sorely tried.

But events moved on and I had to move with them. I could not afford the luxury of sulking over my wounds too long. After about six to eight days in Auschwitz we were trucked yet again, yet again we moved at a slow pace, for two days I believe, before reaching our destination, with no food or drink, just the notorious bucket in the middle of the truck. I remember peering through the ventilation grid and observing the grass banks and flora distinctive of the Bohemian countryside and woodlands. The yearning I experienced then, having forfeited what was justly and rightly mine, having to pass by peering as a prisoner through the grid of a cattle truck, that was another blow. It felt like being carried off on a current too strong to resist and watching the familiar shores and beloved land drift further and further, beyond reach, beyond return. My heart ached ...

Leaving Auschwitz behind was a release from an underworld which normally never let go of its victims. Had we, who had opted to be labourers, beaten the system, broken the spell, or were we being shunted across Europe (as we were later to learn) to be incarcerated in another black hole? I knew, we all knew I am sure, what another Auschwitz would do. Therefore: do not think, nor wonder, nor imagine, nor talk about it. We were silent in the truck, waiting impassively for the journey to end.

Kaufering

NIGHT TIME. THE train has stopped. We are waiting. Then shunting and, presently, the squeal of brakes and the train finally stops.

The doors are rolled back, but there is no shouting, no banging, just a calm order to line up outside. At last we have arrived. We get out and, flanked by armed guards, are marched the short distance to our new prison, the concentration camp of Kaufering near Dachau, one of a number of small camps (in fact ours was number 3, I believe) built no doubt for the specific purpose of expediting an important war project under construction nearby.

I felt immediately that we had come to a different place from Auschwitz. I could sense it even before tasting its realities. As we were soon to find out the Commandant of Kaufering Camp was a man from the Wehrmacht, i.e. from the army, not the SS, who believed in a measure of 'fairness' concerning the 'Jewish solution' scheme, a tall and upright middle-aged man of the old school.

We Czechs were housed in one of three long, low, wooden bunkers set about three feet deep into the ground, inside which was built a raised wooden dais on each side of the long wall to sleep on, or rest, or eat. I believe there could have been up to 50 men to each hut, but we were quite content with our new domicile. The rest of the camp inmates lived in small huts, probably ten men in each.

The regime was definitely milder than in Auschwitz, and more predictable. Apart from the German Commandant and his troops we had an internal executive structure consisting of a number of capos headed by the camp leader directly responsible to the C.C. It was he who organised and disciplined the work squads called commandos which were supervised and guarded by armed soldiers. Most of the work was outside the camp, some plum jobs inside the electrified perimeter fence.

The routine was more than arduous, and under the prevailing conditions with regard to food, shelter, clothing, work and climate, as well as length of internment, and quite apart from hygiene, barely sustainable. Although the food was inadequate, considering the heavy work we were expected to do, it was an improvement on Auschwitz. We were issued black bitter 'coffee' first thing in the morning, and a small portion of bread as we marched out to work later on; then in some work places, cabbage water at midday, and in the evening a large bowl of thick soup and one tiny item such as a spoonful of jam, or a piece of cheese, or a little margarine. To us this seemed to be generous, almost princely, and had it not deteriorated most of us might still have had a chance to last out to the end. This was November 1944; we were freed in April or May 1945 – a long haul. As the food supplies became scarcer, and our rations diminished in quantity and quality, so the death rate among us increased.

Our hut was neither insulated nor heated, of course, and we only had one thin blanket for cover; during the night we huddled together for warmth. Sleeping close to my friends felt cosy and safe, providing the reprieve so urgently needed.

Our clothing differed from those we joined in Kaufering. Their pyjama-striped outfits were a parody of protection against the fierce frosts and icy winds of the Alpine climate we had to battle against. These chiefly Hungarian inmates, with a sprinkling of Poles, suffered the cold more intensely than we did who had been issued, apart from a jacket, trousers and shoes, actual winter coats, possibly because Auschwitz had run out of prison uniforms. Naturally we were the envy of the rest of the prisoners and, being Czech as well, generally unpopular. I certainly did not realise, to begin with, that my heavy coat, which I never left out of sight, was a great treasure and another of my life-savers.

We disliked the Poles and Hungarians because we felt we were unwelcome intruders, and realised they knew all the ropes and therefore had a better chance than us. It only transpired later that the odds were stacked against them because of the length of their confinement and the effect this had on mind and body. But, ultimately, it was the kind of work we were expected to do and the prevailing conditions which determined survival, apart from the psychological factor unique to each individual.

Time was not a measure we possessed, therefore I can only make approximations. We rose sometime, whilst it was pitch dark, to the sound of whistles and, a little later, the arrival of a milk churn outside the entrance full of unsweetened black chicory coffee. Enthusiasm to get out there into the cold for a ladleful or two varied, but I never missed mine, although it meant foregoing five minutes longer under the blanket among my friends. Then roll-call: we rushed out onto the square, the Appellplatz, and stood and waited, and stood and waited – I do not know how long – in groups of one hundred.

On milder mornings this was an ordeal, for we must have stood there for two hours. On cold mornings this was murderous, and when a cold wind blew as well we just did not know how to bear it. But perhaps the worst was driving rain, making us sodden and frozen and desperate, for it seemed that it caused our strength and spirit to seep away even before the march to work and hard labour ahead had begun. But eventually, and to our infinite relief, after having been counted and accounted for, we joined our commandos and dispersed to our specific workplaces.

• • •

Luckily, and I do not remember how it happened, I began work within the camp, assigned to a burly Bavarian and a taciturn Belgian, both drafted by the regime into the Todt organisation as skilled workers, non-Jews living outside the camp. I know that the few weeks I worked with them was yet another life saving situation, for several reasons. I did not have to suffer the long marches to work and back; I had a better midday soup; there was better shelter; there were no armed guards who could be unpleasant, and as I was slowly to realise, the two men were not Nazis. But there were constraints: we hardly ever spoke to each other and I, as prisoner and Jew, felt a division or distance which at times became quite painful. I do believe these men were frightened and had orders not to communicate with a prisoner, but I was not to know this at the time.

It may be that by enjoying the comparative 'luxury' of the situation I had slipped, unconsciously, into a finer mode of existence in which human expectations rise and perceptions become more discriminating. I wanted, oh, I so needed, communication, a sense of belonging, a tiny little sense of worth, some basic equality. I must admit that now and again the burly Bavarian gave a little intimation of it as, for instance, on one occasion, while I was slurping my midday soup straight out of the bowl, sitting a few discreet feet away from the two men, he looked across to me and said, 'Have you no spoon to eat with?' He sounded surprised and somewhat annoyed, so that I believed the fault was mine. 'Don't they even give you spoons?'

Now that was balm to my ears, but also a pain in my heart. A spoon suddenly became a symbol of civilised humanity giving a man his human status. This fellow seemed to acknowledge me as such and attempted to raise me up and out of my acceptance of degradation and rejection from the human fold, yet all he was able to do for me was to promise to bring a spoon the next day, which indeed he did, looking shamefaced.

We performed some joinery tasks around the camp; I, employed as an unskilled apprentice, was ordered to hold this or that piece of timber whilst one of them was sawing it, to fetch or to carry, or to turn the handle of the large old-fashioned grinding stone for sharpening tools. One day I was asked to go to hut eleven to fetch some planks. When I entered a strange odour met me. There were the planks in an untidy heap on the floor, but lying across their ends and in the corner of the hut were several corpses dumped there, waiting, no doubt, for collection and disposal.

There I met death, my grim and relentless enemy, my pursuer since entering Auschwitz, my ultimate fear and horror. Yes, it was death I feared, more than the Nazis, more than humiliation, hunger and deprivation. Death was a totally unacceptable, unthinkable option, a horrible threat I must fight and fight and never give in to. My rejection of death was absolute, and in equal measure my dedication to life – on whatever terms – an irreversible choice.

No such precise thoughts entered my head, for what had gripped my guts, entered my being, was expurgated in a sustained counter-offensive to preserve my spirit to live. I pulled the planks from under the rigid bodies and carried them over to the two men, making two or three journeys. By the time I pulled out the last one the shock had been partly absorbed, my mind busy pushing the horrible discovery behind me.

Our work brought us into the kitchens one week to refurbish a wooden ventilation structure on top of the roof. These sacred halls, filled with stoves and utensils, the smell of cooked food and potato peelings, were strictly out of bounds to prisoners. The sight that met me one day would not ordinarily have been granted to anyone save a capo. There, at the kitchen table, sat a German soldier with a plate of food before him such as I had not seen for over two years: a pork chop with potatoes and vegetable. I stared in resentful disbelief and, momentarily, succumbed to such a violent desire to be given a piece of that meat that I could barely hold on to myself. Like everybody else I tended spasmodically to think about food, such fantasies always connected with home, and quickly dispelled them in order not to make life unbearable. But here was no fantasy, so how would I be able to rid myself of this vision?

Again, a sense of distance, rejection, humiliation, in feeling the way I did. This man and I were light years apart; to me he represented a world outside which I had been banned from, just like the two joiners I worked with. There was no bridge between us, bar the spoon; we were totally separate. The hunger, the kennel I slept in, the shoddy clothes I wore, the wired-in cage I was kept in, the bellowing and threats of the capos, the dirt, lice and senseless hard labour: they all confirmed my inferiority and separation which I was forced to abide by, and suffer, but never, never inwardly to succumb to!

The respite I was granted during this period, when working as an apprentice, was a gift I can only evaluate now. The wounds I had received in Auschwitz could not be healed, but their inevitable bleeding had to be stopped. It must have been then that my thoughts and feelings concerning Paul were being carefully anaesthetised, wrapped in the continual hope of his survival somewhere far away from me. Later, working out in the forests, our marching column met another from some nearby camp, and immediately this hidden hope sprang to life as I looked at each passing man to see if, perchance, Paul was among them.

My shoes began to fall apart, a pair of flimsy town shoes thrown on the counter for me in Auschwitz – no matter if they were too large or too small. It remains one of the numerous mysteries of my camp life as to how I managed to equip myself with a pair of clogs made from off-cuts of planks and material torn from the lining of my winter coat. The alternative was grim: wrapping my feet in rags. This would have meant sacrificing part of my clothing, all of which was indispensable. I dared not imagine the consequences. As it was I shuffled along feeling I was dragging weights on my feet but, at least, I kept going.

Considering how closely we were thrown together, during the evenings (and nights) and on Sundays, I recognise now how little I communicated with my friends, and how very little of what they said – which did not immediately concern me – I really heard. And of all the people in the hut

I only manage to recall two faces! I was aware how much my friends needed all their energy and will to live, but from my perspective they were better able to do so than I was, for they seemed to take on the hardships without flinching or moaning. It makes me wonder how they saw me and whether they, in turn, could understand my predicaments.

Manci, I remember, worked somewhere in the woods, whilst Josch and his brother managed to get work just outside the camp in the military quarters, another plum job. However, my own lucky spell did come to an end when the maintenance work my two joiners performed was completed and I was put into a commando to work outside the camp as well. Harder times still were now upon me.

• • •

The project the Germans were engaged in outside Kaufering defied the wildest fantasy. There in the forest thousands of workers, Todt conscripts and prisoners, as well as Germans, swarmed around the gigantic sites working day and night on what must then have been one of the largest and most powerful constructions ever undertaken. The site we were working on was one of three similar projects and the nearest to completion, part of it already in use.

In choosing the site the Germans had utilised the particular composition of the Bavarian subsoil in the Alpine hinterland where Kaufering is situated, made up, as it is, of gravel and sand reaching great depths, and constituting vital building materials for making concrete structures. To describe the huge design we were working on is not difficult, although the architectural logic is quite beyond my comprehension. Briefly, a large gravel hill was formed in the shape of a cylindrical mound hundreds of feet long, the straight sides reaching down to an unbelievably deep foundation. In other words, the cross-section would resemble an inverted letter U. Six large cement mixing stations with pumping gear were placed three on each side. Day and night section after section of this 'mould' was partitioned and then covered with liquid concrete mixture, working from the foundations upwards to a minimum of seven metres thickness at the top (so I was told by those who knew). When this immense 'crust' was completed several mechanical diggers removed the gravel from under the hardened concrete to reveal the vast hall ready to be utilised. The gravel which had been removed was straightaway transported to the next construction site not far away. The cement necessary to feed the pumping stations was constantly being unloaded from nearby trains arriving daily, the cement being transferred to the mixing stations by some kind of suction system operating by means of piping hidden underground.

Even before completion I saw, down at an amazing depth, dozens of German fighter planes, looking like toys in that vastness, being assembled hurriedly to supply the frantic German war effort. No American or British bomb could penetrate this impervious factory which, even now, standing hidden in the high Bavarian forest, is being used, no doubt, to protect nuclear war-heads and other sensitive war material. This seemed to be the case when I visited the place in the early Eighties in order to show my family where I had slaved during the war. US armed military police with dogs were patrolling along a high perimeter fence, the entrance gate bristling with soldiers who sent us packing without ceremony.

My memory fixes on a few particular 'scenes' and stretches of the forest we either marched through or were working in. I am aware of my feeling for woodlands being very strong ever since childhood, and I believe that something of the solemn beauty of the trees and the mysterious silence around replenished my starved emotions and kept the image alive. Progress along the forest track to get to work was a sluggish shuffle of bedraggled prisoners, flanked by a few armed guards who tried, but failed, to keep the pace moving. Reverie and nostalgia came and went in short and often painful spasms; otherwise there was just numbness, behind which lurked the incessant cry for food and rest.

On leaving the camp in the morning we were issued with our first ration: one slice of cloggy brown bread, our treasure for the day, but also our problem. We never knew which part of the site we were going to work at or what kind of work we would be doing; nor could we know beforehand whether we would be lucky enough to get a ladle of lukewarm cabbage soup at midday. These considerations determined the strategy to be used regarding the ritual disposal of that single modest slice of bread, our minds hovering throughout the whole of the morning stint over this all-important issue. To have the strength of will to keep the bread untouched in the pocket was for me a task beyond my power. As the weeks passed more and more of this life-giving treasure was nibbled away, or altogether eaten, before I held my bowl of cabbage water between my frozen hands. The real trouble came when no 'soup' arrived and my bread was already eaten. A despair which felt like pain overwhelmed me, coupled with a sense of awful guilt of having made a fatal mistake. Yet, at this very moment, I fought against such onslaughts of scruples, forcing myself to adapt to the cruel reality and settle for an image of the forthcoming evening soup. The keen sense of failure on these occasions was reinforced by seeing more strong-minded prisoners tucking into the remains of their morning bread ration. Sharing was out of the question, although it came to mind as a vague hope. The only way of coping was to turn away and change the current of thought, pretend indifference, bury the guilt.

The work consisted mainly of manual digging of improbably deep trenches to house the complex network of enormous pipes which criss-crossed the whole area surrounding the concrete giant. I recall working at such depth that two super-imposed platforms were required to get the stuff to the surface. Pickaxes and long-handled continental style shovels were our tools, an armed guard patrolling within earshot. We also worked on rail construction, on the pumping stations and other projects. Some of us, the doomed, worked night shifts unloading cement.

Marching, or rather, dragging ourselves back to camp was unbelievably wearisome, the only spark in us generated by the prospect of food and rest. But I remember one occasion when I had a conversation with a young Estonian, the talk ranging around 'back home', a flashback to paradisal existence; otherwise the track back was made in silence. Then, or after, lying down in the hut, we did not comment on the day's work, but did discuss the behaviour of the guards. What they did or said had great relevance to our view of the prospects of survival and return, their gesture and expression portents of the coming ending of our ordeal. Hope and illusion, these wavering companions, needed the reassuring stability and indisputable reality of the past; yet sinking too deeply into that world now gone spelled perdition.

The occasional brief glimpse, passing reminiscence, a precious touch of what once was humdrum, everyday, taken-for-granted existence: all these came and fled, as if in terror. But they came back again, not so much to tempt us, more perhaps to give us the balance we needed, to bring some measure of sanity into a warped and incomprehensible situation. It was a matter of retaining a sense of human values, so that, instead of sinking into a morass of self-destructive resignation, we kept our sights on the things that mattered, were self evident, desirable, worth holding out for. The past, in this way, gave meaning by its value to us, and it had to be embraced and celebrated and, for God's sake, restored!

Back at camp meant queuing for soup, our lifeline, taking it back to the hut and flopping down in exhaustion. This was the central focus of the day, the moment we had been waiting for during the dreary and frighteningly long hours working in the cold, during the marches to and from work, these everlasting hours of drudgery: the moment of holding our bowl of hot soup between our hands and the certainty that it was ours to eat. And writing this I see before me the tough little man bargaining with another to exchange one half of his soup for two or three cigarettes. Was it just an unbelievable folly of addiction, or the desperate desire to appease the gnawing hunger with a few puffs, or a brief resurrection of past pleasure? Perhaps it was a combination of all of these. To me this food was holy and totally indivisible, to be incorporated without the loss of a single drop, just like the wine in communion, not merely food but, indeed, a symbol of life everlasting.

This was our time, the time to eat our food, to find comfort in the warmth gradually generated by our bodies, to talk, or to sink into the drowsy half-sleep of extreme tiredness; later to make the effort to sit up and start on the tiresome, and largely ineffective, task of squashing hundreds of lice clinging to our shirts and trousers. In the increasing warmth, sometimes boosted by burning in a little stove the wood we had gleaned and surreptitiously brought back, the lice became active. We itched and scratched and itched and scratched, a quaint torment lasting until sleep gave merciful release.

. . .

Winter became more severe. The ground became frozen and resistant to our attempts to break it with a pickaxe. There is another image which has haunted me all these years, the image of some of the Polish prisoners out there with me in the icy cold, dressed in their quite inadequate blue-striped prison clothes, leaning on their shovel or pickaxe, swaying forward and backward as they mumbled their prayers. They had hardly made an impression on the hardened surface. Their spirit, out of touch with the world around them, had taken over and led them to the shelter of their God, into His sanctuary and His mercy. The guards tended to ignore them.

And I, the young atheist, looked at them in some wonder and disbelief and, yes, with some contempt as well, for 'giving up' in this manner, for pleading for mercy and deliverance through this illusory power they worshipped. My reaction was to hack the ice more fiercely, tax my fading strength to break the hardness at my feet, to succeed in overcoming the waves of fatigue and discounting the meaninglessness of the task. I collaborated? No, I think I was saving my life in making this effort and seeing the result of my labours. There was a spark of pride, a sense of achievement, in this miniscule world of mine which served as a kind of blessing, quite apart from the activity itself which prevented me from being overcome by the creeping cold. These poor men, mostly young (the middle-aged had not survived that long), looked altogether spent: hollow cheeked, thin, frozen blue, their eyes fixed at a distant point, expressionless, beyond communication. Seeing them there as they were swaying to and fro, their lips forever moving in prayer, we knew they were swiftly moving toward the end of their journey. We had a name for them: Muselman. They were the next in line.

More powerful than anything was the almost ferocious determination not only to avoid becoming a 'Muselman' (one who has lost the fight) myself, but also not to be seen as one. A look, a word from any one, would have been tantamount to final condemnation and execution. Despite the appalling condition we found ourselves in I believe the crucial battles were fought within, and he who gave up his fight had only days left to live. And here I am left wondering how these men felt: did they feel lost or forsaken, or were they mercifully embraced in their last hours and peacefully led away? I believe both conditions prevailed, in that order.

Sundays were rest days; that is, if we were not under some punishment and forced out to work around the camp. We still had to stand for ages on the Appellplatz to be counted and accounted for, although not for as long as on work days. But Sunday is remembered for another thing: the coffee.

By some strange quirk of mentality emanating from the highest echelons of the camp hierarchy, coffee was dispensed to us on Sundays containing milk and sugar! The piping hot elixir became another communion in worship attended by all without exception, unlike the bitter black stuff barely enticing a trickle of devotees. This, instead, left a warm glow in mind and body for the rest of the morning at least. Never mind that the coffee was brewed from chicory, the sugar probably saccharin, the milk tinned; this extra, this bonus, this gift, was never lost on me. This tiny affirmation, this gentle little stroke, acted like a healing touch to my stricken soul, fuelling renewed hope and promise, ameliorating for a while the deep-seated pain. What hours of consoling talk will not achieve, a small gesture, a glance, a smile will.

Well do I remember a grey and frosty London morning in a slummy bed-sitter in Kilburn, one year hence, on a day which promised nothing except the next meal, nights riddled with nightmares, and yet another grey day.

'You don't know Nes coffee?'

'No.'

'Would you like some?' 'I don't know. Perhaps.'

The aroma was devastating, the taste out of this world. I did not make the connection then; that came many years later. I just did not know myself. I was lost.

• • •

It was a sunny Sunday in Kaufering which lured me into an apparently harmless decision that nearly cost me my life. A winter's day treacherously warm and of invigorating effect. My ration of coffee earlier may have been a contributing factor, too. In any case, I decided to have a wash and try to scrub my louse-infested shirt with the help of a tiny piece of hard brown soap, issued to us but hardly ever used. The wash hut near the centre of the compound had but few visitors and I performed my ablutions and my washing in absolute privacy. It only occurred to me afterwards that I had no way of drying my shirt except by fixing it above my sleeping place during the day, keeping it under observation, and lying on top of it during the night.

The following day was a disaster. I had to put on a damp shirt and stand for ages in the cold. To my dismay we marched out into freezing gusts of wind and I clearly remember standing near the edge of some woods and overlooking an immense plain thinly covered in drifting snow blown about by icy winds. I think I did pray then for the shirt to dry out quickly and I wondered and doubted if I would get through that day. It certainly was one of the longest days in my life, and one of the most costly ones.

Another time in the wash hut. The sirens wailed in alarm one Sunday and I stayed put to observe an Allied raid on Munich and Augsburg. The sound of the high flying fortresses was heavenly music to my ears, the rumble of distant explosions an intoxicating foretaste of release from bondage. Alas, I could also see the sudden black smoke in the sky as one and another of the planes was hit, and I recall the instant fear of failure this seemed to indicate, the direct hits exposing the vulnerable aspect of Allied forces. Would they ever make it? Will they be in time? How much longer are we to wait, how much longer?

We lived between the soup and Allied attacks now, the two only hopes. The attacks became more frequent, but the soups grew thinner.

One day an event occurred which awakened in me a momentary uplift and sense of power in stark contradiction to my condition. One of the numerous air-raid alarms turned into the nasty reality of an air attack on our work site. The distant rumble of approaching planes was a matter of indifference to us prisoners, but not so to the German soldiers and Todt workers around us who knew better. Suddenly there were shouts and yells and commands from all sides and a wild scramble for the nearest available shelter. The site emptied as I listened in wonder to the noise of engines and the sputter of machine-gun fire and saw the few small US fighter planes strafing the woodlands. Friends at last! Tiny friends come to help us! It felt good, strangely good. I wished it would last. I became aware of calls and screams directed at me, but I was in no mood to run for it. I had seen the guards running, rifles and all, and I felt scorn for them, I almost pitied their apparent cowardice. It was then that I experienced that sense of power, holding my life in my hands in face of such danger. How different it was for once to have a choice, so profoundly satisfying. An irrational thought made me believe that, in any case, these bullets were not meant for me, therefore would not hit me. And there was also elation in the other possibility that they might, nevertheless, do just that, and this risk awoke some deeply intrinsic instinct from an archaic past. I walked calmly into the shelter among abuse and insults which, however, did not touch me, for once. Something bigger had touched me instead.

The German Wehrmacht Commander of the camp was relieved of his duties and apparently sent to the Eastern Front for being too lenient. We feared the worst and unfortunately were proved right, for his replacement was an SS brute, a fat, uncouth, red-faced creature bent on 'tightening the discipline' and 'tightening the belt'. Apart from that, supplies were deteriorating and diminishing as the Allied front was pushing forward and the main supplies for the camp, potatoes and bread, were affected by the frost and mildew respectively. Priority was, of course, given to the military to keep up their morale, thus reducing our pitiful rations. The soldiers' indoctrination classes were hyped up with a noticeable increase of nastiness towards us. Punishments for minor transgressions of rules intensified, dire threats bawled across the Appellplatz in the mornings, with occasional public beatings which sometimes proved fatal, if not immediately, then within a few days. In our condition brutal attacks of that kind were beyond our strength.

One of us, the man who slept right next to the door on the left side of our hut, would not get up one morning. He was a swarthy, dark-haired, stocky fellow, probably a farmer, possibly in his late thirties. Roll call was absolutely obligatory and we had to stand outside or be taken to the dreaded infirmary, a hut for the dying. The whistle went and, after much prompting and pulling, we tried to manhandle him out on to the square. But he resisted with incredible stubbornness. He had also dirtied himself. He was like a lump of stone; he was immovable. We knew he would receive a dreadful beating or finish in the infirmary, so we tried our best. But he had given up and it was all the same to him what happened next. It was almost as though his spirit had departed and only the heavy hulk of his body was lying there to be used by others at will, any-old-how. He was carried away and we never saw him again.

• • •

Then Manci fell ill

Manci, my youth leader, the man of the world: tough, the down-to-earth no nonsense man, a manual worker most of his life, his lovely wife Ženka in some camp somewhere. Manci caught the fever and struggled to keep going. But his strength eventually failed him and he went down with pneumonia.

This hit us badly, not only because he was the strongest among us, but because people who went into the infirmary did not usually return, they were disposed of. We feared for him. Joschka, who knew about his condition in the infirmary, was very perturbed, telling us the fever was not coming down, and he was going to try his luck with the soldiers he was working for; a risky move indeed!

Two days later, however, he came in beaming: he had obtained some medicine, and he was going to get it through to Manci. It took a few more days, but then a gradual improvement in Manci's condition took place, and not long afterwards came his release. We rejoiced, although he still looked quite dreadful and was feeling very weak.

This was almost a miracle, and in more than one sense. Not long after Manci's illness, on a Sunday again, we were put under strict orders to stay in our huts. Then all the patients from the infirmary were taken into the square, some of them being carried out, and made to sit or lie in a circle on the ground. There must have been two or three dozen people in various conditions of sickness and enfeeblement. There they sat, apparently impassive, waiting.

Three or four army trucks arrived, armed guards jumped out and surrounded the patients. Their officer talked to the camp Commander. Then the patients were loaded into the back of the lorries and the cavalcade drove out of the camp. And that was that: human fodder for the insatiable gas chambers, meek, resigned, without protest.

No, not quite. I remember peering out of our hut and noticing, before the trucks arrived, one or two of the patients trying to edge away from the circle, sliding on their bottoms, in the vain hope of getting away from what they knew was going to happen. Because it was such a pathetic manoeuvre, so utterly futile, it struck a strange chord within me. It may be I sensed the proximity of that crucial fork where a choice is made, not on a conscious level, between reason and madness. The scene I witnessed could be a charade projected by my mind for some insane personal entertainment. But the circle of prisoners on the ground was real! The mind enters a dimension beyond comprehension, gropes about, loses itself in twisted corridors of irrationality, and I, laughing out loud, might burst out from the hut to join the ring of those to be executed.

My choice was to harden my heart yet again, steel my nerves, barely allow a meagre pity to move me as a shoddy token to the atrocity before me. What counted more than anything was the wish for this moment to pass away, for the loaded trucks to depart and never to return, for this episode to be forgotten, the fight for life resumed.

• • •

Life ground on, day after day, week in week out. Rumour about the approaching Allied armies was confused and uncertain; inadequate, in fact, to raise our hopes sufficiently. My strength was seeping away, I was bowed down by the weight of lethargy probably typical of our condition, obvious to any outsider. Within myself the mists were lying low, now and again lifting a little when some event or change took place. Otherwise life filtered through a kind of screen and my response to it was mechanical and minimal. I lived in my self-protected world, not communicating nor relating, a limbo existence which continued throughout many post-war years. It began and took hold of me here in Kaufering, when I was forced to default on my humanity and to seek solace and phoney security within a brittle encrustation of my own making.

None of this was conscious. As the level of existence fell lower and lower, and with it my physical and mental condition, conscious participation also diminished, and at its lowest must have reached the level of animal functioning. Things happened to me, I was being happened. I had been starved into submission. I had been set apart, away from the place I belonged. All connection had been severed. And in this each of us was utterly alone.

No description will illuminate this situation, no explanation can reveal the nature of such an existence. I mention it and let it pass with the realisation that I am failing in the task I set myself when embarking on this writing. So often I hear it said that an experience was so horrific it was like living hell. Indeed, the transport and arrival and the days spent in Auschwitz were living hell, for me and everyone, without exception. There was then still enough life in us, enough spirit, to experience hell for what it was, despite hurriedly mobilised psychological defences to fight and protect ourselves with. Then the mists were not there, the encrustation only just begun, our vulnerability clearly visible in eyes and expression, our engagement conscious and fanatical.

Not so now. Too much had happened and any fight available had been beaten out of us. And I, for one, lived – subsisted – in a manner which disallowed past or future to impinge, merely leaving the bare present as the only means to continue. The variety and richness of ordinary human awareness, although never fully realised, was radically amputated so as to leave only the barest fraction necessary to exist within the immediate here and now.

The essence of 'when?' is to relate backwards or forwards. 'When was it?' or 'when was I?', 'when will it?' or 'when will I?' are past or future orientated, each dimension allowing endless scope. Equally the essence of 'why?' and, 'how?' brings past or future into the present, adding meaning and purpose, creating further dimensions. We do this habitually, incidentally, casually, intuitively, becoming philosophical only by intention. These dimensions are part and parcel of the human condition, inscribed into our soul, basic means of operating in the world. But they had been taken away from us.

The mental state I was in did not rescue me from the profound shock I suffered one morning when I was pulled out of my work squad and planted among the depleted lines of the notorious night-shift squad. I was suddenly shaken out of my stupor into a renewed agony of knowing my life-line had been cut, my hopes of survival, so secretly harboured, mercilessly dashed. As I was made to stand in the front line of my team, the German guard in charge of us came straight at me and hit me on my face, shouting: 'You fat Jewish pig!' The irony escaped me; it is possible my face was more rounded, better preserved perhaps, maybe bloated. The blow merely symbolised my latest predicament, dragging me further into the abyss.

My new quarters were in one of the small huts and I was among men I did not know and, since they were Hungarian, I could not understand. My link with my friends was broken and I could not cope with that. The pain and sorrow were so acute that the tears kept welling up but I had no tears to cry with. I realised, besides, that my fate had been sealed, as if I had suddenly found myself in the circle in the middle of the square, waiting for disposal. Something had snapped inside and the will to fight had received a mortal blow.

We marched out into the night to the awe-inspiring site lit by innumerable spot-lights and teeming with activity. I could have marched to my execution; my hopelessness and dejection were complete. And how I ever coped that night with the work I had to do is beyond my comprehension. We were ordered to unload trucks full of cement bags from a train standing along a platform, and carry these heavy weights into the large warehouse nearby which had a big iron grid fixed into the floor. Onto this the bags were emptied and the cement was immediately absorbed underground by means of a suction system.

I tried all manner of means to negotiate the bags between truck and grid: on my shoulders, on my back, holding it in front. They were heavy, ever so heavy, and they grew heavier as the night wore on. The last remaining dregs of strength drained away that night and I knew my end was near. I could not be expected to manage what other prisoners before me had failed in, yet I had to keep on my feet, move and carry and not collapse.

If ever there were men broken we belonged among them, walking with them the path of no return. This was the end at last, not to be reckoned in terms of days, only of hours. If I survived this night, I certainly could not survive the next. There is a truly weird sense of unreality about the end of that shift, amnesia about the march back, but a clearer memory of staying among strange men in a strange hut, separated from my friends, utterly alone. It must have happened during this darkest of nights that I committed my crime of stealing one or two tiny potatoes from a metal container, belonging to one of the sleeping men, which I saw hanging on a nail on the wall.

Thus a sense of moral degradation added to my physical and mental disintegration.

The following day is totally lost to me. But not the following night. Recently there had been alerts and bombing raids of increased frequency, but we had become used to it, ceased to see it as a sign of approaching freedom. The war activity had become irrelevant. But that night the incredible miracle happened: we arrived to see an empty platform, no train, no cement. Ordered to wait, and told it would arrive later, we sat around counting every single minute of rest as a heaven-sent blessing.

An hour passed, then two, then three. No train came. 'Of course it will come!' we were told, 'no doubt about that!' And so we waited and gained a night of rest. Not mental rest, though, for the fear of the expected train rolling in kept us in a state of extreme suspense.

But that night the train did not arrive, nor the next night, nor the one after that. The cement supply had ceased, and so, I believe, the construction process, centred around the mighty mixing and pumping stations. Each night added a tiny bit of strength to our spent bodies, added a spark of hope. This was an unprecedented event – how much, then, dare we hope?

These nights of anxious waiting are lodged deeply somewhere in my mind, revealed only through odd fragments of scenes and moods rather than happenings. A strange expectancy, a strange stillness was hovering uneasily, a strange sense of unseen forces beyond good and evil gathering beyond my vision, decreeing what is to be and to become. How long, how many nights we waited I cannot tell. We were not to know that this was the pause before the final act, the hush before the curtain rises ...

• • •

One day the long column was formed without much fuss. Our bread ration issued we proceeded out of camp on a march the meaning of which I barely speculated on. Manci, Joschka and his brother were somewhere in the long column and that felt alright, and the issue of bread had been very welcome, but also reassuring, because condemned men assigned to the gas chambers would not be given precious bread to eat. Or would they?

Of course there was no certainty, there never had been, these months. I sensed the precariousness of our situation as we walked slowly along the country roads towards an unknown destination, and as the hours passed the little energy saved during the previous nights off work was being used up bit by bit, with nothing to replace it. My clumsy wooden clogs were becoming intolerably heavy, but it was the inner emptiness which sapped the motivation to carry on. My body and mind pleaded for rest – now, forever. But on and on we went, slower and slower, despite the shouts and threats of the guards, with nights' rests I do not know where.

One place I do remember, though, very clearly indeed.

The edge of a wood, with fields stretching far and wide, a beautiful spring evening with the sun setting in a golden glow, a short rest period to be terminated soon in order to march on and on again. I lie stretched out with eyes closed, the vision of so much beauty pervading my whole being, and a sense of approaching slumber which I prayed might lead me out of this world, taking this vision with me. I longed, then, more fervently than I ever longed for anything, to be left there, to be forgotten and allowed to approach my end my own way, just like this, alone, at peace. I knew that sleep would lead me out, that all would be well, if only I was allowed to stay.

More shouts, commands, somebody shaking me back into the unacceptable bruising present. Then onto my sore feet, and shuffle again, each step a supreme effort.

Something happened the following day, a new situation arose, the significance of which took time to sink into my dulled mind. Our guards had vanished! A thousand or more prisoners dragged themselves along the empty country road without altering course, without breaking ranks and dispersing into fields and woodlands. Manci and the Gold brothers had joined me by now and we consulted together briefly and in great excitement.

'They'll shoot us if they see us getting away?'

'You don't know, they may be waiting somewhere to see what we are up to; that would give them an excuse.'

'Even if they have gone, where can we go?'

'Better to stay together!'

We stayed together, and marched on and on. Perhaps some of us made off; I am not sure of that.

Allach

IN THE LATE AFTERNOON we came to what had presumably been planned to be our destination, which only our camp leader would have known about, and we marched ourselves into our last concentration camp without being harassed or ordered about, a wretched horde of wrecked humanity. The gate stood open, guard posts were deserted, and the building which was obviously the Commandant's headquarters stood empty, the doors open for anyone to enter. But we had no curiosity whatsoever, we had only one desire at that moment: to stop walking, to sink down, and to rest.

A camp official appeared and directed us to our quarters, a few large empty huts with some ancient blankets on the concrete floor: We were told this was Allach, a camp near Munich, at least double the size of Kaufering. The soldiers had left the previous day, we were informed. There may have been some food that evening, but I am not sure. In any case, in my state this was less important than to be able to lie down and doze, and especially not to be expected to move or do anything. I was in a comatose state, with but one concern: how to find the Herculean strength to get myself to the latrine. There was no support or help available, it was each man for himself. Losing control of this most basic and private function was tantamount to letting go altogether, like the man in our hut not long before. It would have meant a point of no return, and I was still clinging to life.

How many days passed I cannot tell, nor when the shooting started. Was it the following day, or the day after? 'They are coming!' was what flashed through my mind, and everybody else's.

'They are here!' people were shouting. We realised a decisive moment was at hand, the direct hits on our camp incontrovertible evidence, but we knew not who was coming, which army was closing in on us.

It was true. This was no longer a rumour, this was for real. The shooting did not last long, but made the whole place shake. There followed a long period of silence, and, on our part, expectant and apprehensive waiting. I was quite awake now, listening to the men around me guessing and arguing the meaning of all this, making predictions about what was going to happen. Why shoot at the camp? And since we were the target, why did it stop?

The old conflict arose again, an alerted instinct calling for caution against premature jubilation. 'Hold back!' and 'Wait and see!' But then the infectious stir around me, and the awakening powerful stir within of deprived and denied desires, roused me beyond belief, screaming to be let out to rampage ...

At last the unbearable suspense gradually turned to jubilation as one after another of the tougher prisoners, who had gone out to see for themselves, reported spotting US soldiers! It was sometime later that we heard that the German anti-aircraft gun, situated right next to the perimeter fence, had been silenced, causing a number of fatal casualties among the prisoners.

Now I could allow, at long last, my inner conflict to subside. But instead of a wild frenzy of joy, and tears of relief, thanksgiving and gladness, I was to start on another long and weary journey leading, as it were, out of an Egypt of slavery, between the threatening and towering walls of seas just held back to let me pass, pursued by the demons of past experience, into an unknown land of the future. A journey of more than forty years, and yet to be completed. It must have started there, on my filthy blankets in Allach, a prisoner freed but not free, degraded, bound in confusion; though his ultimate wish seemingly fulfilled, yet drifting into a vacuum, wandering into some kind of no-man's-land, in perverse completion of what the enemy had failed to achieve.

Moments of potential ecstasy can be moments of potential calamity. When ecstasy rests on dream fulfillment, reality enters to demolish the dream. Did I dimly sense that any joy, let alone ecstasy, was not to be mine, that it could never be reached and embraced? If reality was not to destroy me the price for my life must be paid through a column obligation: the abandonment of joy. To redeem the past was my work, to redeem the guilt of being a survivor I had to carry the burden of joylessness.

None of this was in any way formed in my mind at the time, floundering, as it was, incapable of concentration, devoid of interest. Another part of me began to engage to meet the extraordinary changes that took place, imperceptibly consolidating a framework from the chaos of conflicting emotions flooding my conscious self. It must have happened here, at this most important moment of my life, that a change took place within which led me far beyond my old self and, alas, by many devious and erroneous routes, to a space which I believe is mine.

Our camp was under the control of the US army when some extraordinary things happened which makes me think that their shooting was better than their skill in caring. I was still prone on the floor of the hut when the proclamation was issued giving us permission to leave the compound and feel free to settle our score with the German civilians living in the vicinity of the camp. The mentality responsible for such a crazy idea must have been that of a retarded teenager brainwashed by Hollywood Westerns, and should, in fairness, have provided us with the required Colts to accomplish the proposed vendetta! It was sticks and fists which had to make do, and the toughies of the camp, followed by those less able but still strong enough to sally forth, ranged through the countryside causing havoc and panic among innocent people. We were given three days, and I have no conception what happened throughout this madness. I suppose an army boss must have read a psychological study on the need of prisoners like ourselves to be given the means of release of suppressed anger!

Another grievous mistake was caused by what 1 can only describe as the 'bigger the better' syndrome. To turn the tide, to reverse our fortunes, to get us fit in body and cheered in mind, we were given delicious soups by courtesy of the US forces stores – laced with meat and fat, an incredibly satisfying and quite irresistible potion. As can be imagined the effect on our starved bodies was absolutely disastrous. Within the day the majority of prisoners succumbed to a form of diarrhoea causing the death of numbers of us at the very dawn of their hard-won freedom.

Clearly I speak out of anger, seemingly unaware that I owe my life to those I am maligning, apparently disregarding their sacrifices and losses. Indeed they suffered too, but it seems to me that the losses we then sustained through avoidable mismanagement and macho attitudes are unforgivable, as is the mentality of revenge, more than matched by some of the Russian soldiery raping and plundering in the aftermath of glorious victory.

None of my friends had any intention of joining in the violent vendetta spree. When the three days had passed, during which many a 'success story' was gleefully related by some of our fellow prisoners, a warning from the military came into operation: anyone to leave camp would be shot at without warning. One or two did just that and were carried back wounded.

In the meantime Manci and Joschka had befriended an important Czech capo who offered us accommodation in the stores hut in return for transport duties around the camp. This meant pushing a medium-sized old-fashioned hand cart, loaded at the kitchens with large churns of food for distribution in the camp, as well as carting other supplies. We also transported typhoid patients out of their wrecked hut, hit by one of the shells, into an isolation unit established by the new command. I tried at first to help with these chores.

The new quarters were unbelievable bliss. the greatest gift received since our departure from Terezín: privacy, space, but also unlimited food supplies, lots of extras such as goodies standing on shelves of the store-hut left behind by the retreating soldiers. To earn this immense privilege I tried to join in pushing the cart, but failed to keep going, although I could hold on and be propelled forward by the momentum created by my friends pushing that much harder.

I felt useless; I could not really stand up properly and was told without ceremony to go back and stay in the hut, keeping the door locked. This was a precaution ordered by the capo who had given us our commission.

And so I lay there for many days whilst Manci and the Golds went on their trips, returning to rest, chat and eat several times during the day. Even so I felt marginalised, and the obvious conclusion that they were in better shape than I was did not help. An additional factor, relating to my physical condition, was the extraordinary side-effect of fits of suffocation I experienced every time I ate more than a morsel of food. To resist the temptation to eat that little bit more, to eat all the time in fact, was too hard for me, especially as I was surrounded by outrageous amounts of food and all the leisure to enjoy it. I was almost mindless and I lived in a strange vacuum only broken by my attempts to get some food into me. So I ate and I suffocated, the spasms at times so acute that I thought my end had come. Nevertheless, I gradually began to pick up energy, my jaunts to the wash and toilet hut becoming less of a Herculean effort, the spasms less severe.

One day I was given the task of taking our eating bowls for a good scrub. On the way to get this done a big fellow approached me, saw the bowls, grabbed them from me and walked away without a backward glance, leaving me near to tears and profoundly shaken. A new enemy had emerged, a bestial creature from within our midst, without a heart, brutal, evil. I could hardly bear this, nor did I know how to tell my friends. How could I possibly hold my head up when I told them the unlikely tale of losing our bowls without even a fight. Here was proof of my feebleness and incompetence I could not deny, and I felt beaten.

Eating bowls were an almost sacred symbol representing the continuance of our existence; my failure to defend them and letting them go was an act of treachery. Also, if this was to be the new present, what was I to expect next, what was it worth? From where this aggression came more was to come, I thought. Thus a fresh fear lodged within me seeking permanent abode. This had been an unpropitious beginning to the new future, the future so eagerly, no, so greedily craved.

My friends said little, though, but looked rather incredulous. I, of course, felt condemned. but the feeling did not last too long. Another set was soon provided and the incident was closed.

The days at Allach were nearing their end, rumours of repatriation running riot. With the gradual return of our strength the desire to go home grew also, turning into impatience and even anger. Little did we know about what was going on out there beyond the fence, about the retreating German armies, the minor revolutions staged to clear large areas of the remains of Nazi supremacy. Uncertainty, confusion, and the absence of reliable information – old bed-fellows we knew well – suddenly became a source of frustration hard to contain in our longing for an end to all this, for a new beginning. We needed to engage on our own terms at last, in a place of our choice, free of the junk of the past and, most of all, free to search out our dear ones wherever they were and hopefully alive, to reunite with, and to live!

It was in May that the green German Wehrmacht uniforms were distributed to us hurriedly, the trucks ready for our departure home. The previous days had been filled with speculation on how repatriation would be organised, if at all. Who would be able to leave? What would be the best way to get home sooner than the others? Should we pretend to be Poles or Russians, Austrians, Germans or Czechs? We could have wangled any of these options, as I was to wangle a few months later in a different context.

In any case, we stayed 'Czech' and we were one of the first to climb onto the open army trucks and move out of Allach. We were given a raw egg each for the journey, an unusual and perhaps symbolic ration. It was an object of wonder as well as some amusement, and the problem of how to consume it without any loss became the subject of animated interchanges as we drove along.

Our route took us through Munich, now in ruins, singed and shattered remains of high buildings pointing accusing fingers skyward, the rubble below an unending graveyard. But I was unmoved, merely curious, with not a fibre in me stirred to pity, or even a little sympathy. Such notions had to wait until later to impinge on the mind. My emotions then stayed cold, indifferent.

Pilsen was our destination, not a long or arduous journey to make, and from there by train, in real carriages this time, to Prague.

I leant out from the window of the moving train with increasing trepidation in my heart.

Prague

What was I to expect?
What was I to find?
What would happen?

A MAELSTROM OF contradictory feelings engulfed me, a mixture of anxiety and joy welling up indiscriminately. The time had perhaps come to begin to see the enormity of what had happened to me – since thinking about it was now permitted – and no better time than on this train rolling towards Prague and home, suspended as I was between an abysmal past and a beckoning future. The force of those feelings is indescribable, suppressed emotions rising like flames of fire threatening to engulf me.

And the flicker of hope, not extinguished since Auschwitz, was there in among all this turmoil: Paul! Perhaps ... Might he ...?

But the old Censor came to my rescue yet again, inner warnings damping the fervour and calling for caution. Not yet! Wait! Patience!

We form odd notions about what it feels like to be freed, simplistic and sentimental ideas of a spirit let out of a cage to fly towards new life, ruptures of feelings, tears of relief, a happy return back to where one has always belonged, embraces of welcome, and so on. Perhaps this is how those who are eagerly awaiting the return of the 'prodigal son' would like it to be, expecting him, who has at long last returned, to fit in with what is, in their view, only proper: due gratitude, joy, relief. And perhaps fragments of these are present, but, sadly, so are other less attractive ingredients: doubt and estrangement, for instance, a persistent reserve and, apparent to the keen observer, an air of assumed interest and enthusiasm hiding the underlying all-pervading pain.

For the world has moved on and has changed in his absence, the image of 'home' which had kept him going replaced by a new reality which fits him little and suits him less.

How was I to know all that as I was moving headlong into the ambiguous arms of my future? There in the train the mind worked feverishly, expectancy rising to dangerous limits, warning bells ringing in between.

The train rumbled into the Prague station at last and I see myself on the streets of Prague, my beloved town and birthplace, dressed in my German uniform, on a beautiful sunny day, quite bemused, but with one single thought in my mind: Go to aunt Edith! Will she be there?

I stepped into a crowded no. 11 tram, the same old tram I had always used and been so fond of, to take me up to Vinohrady, where we had also lived before internment, only to realise that I had no money for the fare. But the conductor waved my pleading apology aside and wished me a happy homecoming. I must have looked a convincing Nazi victim despite the uniform.

Was aunt Edith still living in Habánská street? And uncle Willy? And if not, how on earth would I ever be able to find them? The tension inside me reached breaking point when I found the house, got up to the second floor, and rang the bell. My sister-in-law M. opened the door, aunt Edith almost immediately behind her.

'Otto! Otto is here!'

'But where is Paul? You were together?'

'Where IS Paul?'

Yes, there were hugs, there were tears, and there was uncle looking much older and worn; Edith, as lively as ever, talking and asking and asking again, and hurting, and driving the nail deeper into me. The supreme moment went stone cold, and I found myself again in an iron grip of loss, grief and guilt, inescapable feelings gripping tightly like a cramp, immobilising and destructive.

I entered a world of pain which had been successfully kept at bay for so long, but now emerged in full force. I was but one among so very many who were fated to live in such a way, only my pain belonged to me so deeply that I could find no means of sharing it.

Edith's flat became my new 'home'; a place I had of course known, but had never felt comfortable in as a visitor, owing to the frequent disagreements and quarrels between my parents and my aunt. My uncle, a Sudeten German and non-Jew, had always been held suspect of being a Germanophile and sympathetic to German nationalistic aspirations, whilst Edith was not above the occasional family intrigue. Relations between 'them' and 'us' swung wildly, from big bust-ups to great emotional reunions.

This had not been lost on me and came to mind as I accepted Edith's and Willy's hospitality, or, to be more accurate, submitted myself to it. The days and weeks of my stay there come back to me with particular poignancy as a stage in my life where some big issues, not recognised as such, were shaping my life and determined important decisions I made, again, without being aware of their importance.

To start with, I slipped into the unused-to and superb comforts of a humdrum middle-class way of life as easily as I slipped under the luscious duvet that first night in the flat. The way I took this sudden reversal of life-style for granted amazes me now. Here I was at Edith's, in lovely Prague which I always claimed to be my city, looked after with regard to shelter, food and family care. I ought to have been more than content with this.

But soon after arrival, even on that first day, I believe, there came the shock which took my breath away.

'Paul has come back,' we heard. 'Someone said he had come back!'

This message was far too big for me, and inwardly I was beside myself. 'If this is true? Could it be true? Wait! Don't believe it yet!' And so on. It was nothing less than cruel; a brainless thing to do. As it turned out somebody else called Paul had returned. This awful mistake was like a delicate confirmation that he would never return, as though a false affirmation were a double negation to my last fragile hope.

My physical condition was poor. I could walk, eat my food, fitfully absorb what was going on around me, but my ability to sustain any physical effort was severely restricted. Adding to this I would guess that my mind was deeply traumatised. Into this condition of general disability Edith stepped in with determination and resolve. I was to settle outstanding debts owed to my family by various 'friends' with whom we had deposited large amounts of domestic items, to await our return once the war was over. Edith harangued me daily, no doubt with the best intentions, over the urgent need to get back a whole lot of stuff, some of it very valuable. In her view all it needed was that bit of grit on my part to get back what undoubtedly belonged to me.

'You owe it to your father!' she would say. 'He worked hard enough for it all his life. The least you can do is to get going, see these people, and arrange for the things to be returned. You could bring some of it back yourself.'

This became my daily diet for some time to come, and, without mincing her words, she made me feel feeble. However, there was no way I could communicate my inner upheaval and disorientation to her, my sense of dejection, the sheer physical exhaustion.

Even so I tried; but without any conviction. My heart was not in it. And when my missions ended in failure my aunt's anger rose and my depression deepened. I did, on one occasion, come back with a suitcase, but that was it.

'Sorry. This is all we have for you,' I was told, knowing it was untrue.

'Now listen here,' the intimate solicitor friend of my father told me, 'I myself have been sent to the concentration camp like you. Can't you see it? Look at my hair! Look at me!' His hair was shorn, he was much slimmer than he had been. 'This has happened because of you. I should never have done this for your family!'

He said he had been imprisoned because of us. I did not believe a word of this, of course. I could only think of the large double garage below his sumptuous house full of our antique furniture, oil paintings, silver, glass, and the gorgeous and cherished French bikes Paul and I had been given by our father.

Not only had the living links with my dearest ones been severed, but the last remnants of our material household had been grabbed from me. I had no weapon against such determined and clever manipulation; I just caved in, humiliated for having to ask, and coming away empty handed. Worse was to come when I returned to Edith's place. There was no end to the barbed nagging and challenges to make me go on trying. There was even a trip to town, I remember, to consult my aunt's solicitor. By now 1 had lost trust in solicitors and I just stood by while Edith did all the talking. In the end nothing came of it.

It is hard for me to explain why I came to undertake the journey to Terezín in order to claim back my piano, except that it must have meant more to me than other things. It did not seem to occur to me that, even if I got it back, I had no place to accommodate it or play it! There was no logic in this, I acted by sheer impulse.

Terezín was now a refugee camp, and a place for former inmates waiting to be repatriated. Getting in was not easy since the Russians were in charge and all the entrances into the Ghetto were guarded. I parleyed in Czech to explain I had been an inmate myself and that I was claiming my piano! This extraordinary request must have been sufficiently farfetched to impress the guards and to let me through.

How one incentive leads to new openings became clear when I started my inquiries in the children's home I had lived in. Here I met a former chemistry teacher of mine, Willy Groag, who was living there with his wife and children (it astonishes me how they had all survived; it was one of the few miracles for a whole family to be reunited). He informed me that the former secretary of the home, whom I remembered well, had taken my piano back to Germany. This made me really angry and I decided to get my own back by swiping the best piano in the place, a lovely and almost new

Bösendorfer baby grand I had often listened to and knew where to find.

Before attempting this abduction Willy Groag told me that he was in charge of an international scheme to gather young orphans to emigrate abroad. Would I like to do that, for he was able to arrange it for me? I said I did not know, and I must have looked quite switched off about it. Where would I like to go, he went on, undismayed. He could send me anywhere in the world, and he proceeded to list all the countries I could go to. I was still switched off, but when he said England I heard myself say: 'Yes.'

'England?' he said. 'Why England?'

'I don't know,' I said truthfully. I had reacted intuitively and could not explain. I would have found uncles and aunts in the US, in England was a cousin I hardly knew. But why probe?

'I'll let you know when to come for the medical. By the way, I am putting you down as German, and you are fifteen years old, remember.'

'Fifteen? But I am twenty-one.'

'You'll say you are fifteen. Otherwise it's off.'

I believe it was Willy who produced a document for me which served as entitlement to take possession of 'my' piano. Next day I presented my document to the Russians and took myself to the nearest village to negotiate for some transport to get the grand out of Terezín.

It makes me shudder to think of a precious instrument being manhandled onto a hay wagon by rough and ready means and jolted on a bad road to the farm and put in a primitive outhouse. And I still wonder at the energy I suddenly found to get all this done within the space of a few hours.

Back at Edith's I resumed my life of unfocused, indeterminate inactivity typical of slow convalescence, my mind detached from the recent exploits. Then Edith went away with uncle, on their usual round to collect black-market foodstuffs from the country, providing a welcome break from her persistent demands I was incapable of satisfying.

During that time, on one of my walks near our flat, and still wearing my German uniform, I was accosted by an attractive young German girl in a state of acute terror. She needed help, she said. She was being pursued by Czech nationalists still engaged in purging Prague of Nazi elements in hiding. I shall never forget her fearful face, and my helplessness and miserable indecision. Suddenly, out of the blue, the 'other side' was in dire need, and I just could not manage to switch from one over-determined position to a new situation, from victim to rescuer. And so I shook my head and walked away, leaving her standing in her helpless fear. I know now that anything could have happened to her then as the Czechs, puffed up with sudden heroism and revolutionary zeal, were using gross violence, by preference, to prove their manhood, to assuage the merciless demands of age-old hatreds. The guilt of deserting this girl has never left me.

The call for my medical examination came, and I took the train to Terezín not really believing anybody would be mad enough to send me cost-free to a country of my choice, to settle there for life. I was ambivalent about staying in my country of birth, equally ambivalent about leaving it.

What did spur me on was another blow: receipt of papers requiring my attendance at an enlistment procedure for conscription into the army! This surely was an outrage. I could, at that stage, hardly walk a quarter of a mile without exhaustion, I still found it difficult to sit on a chair for longer than five minutes because of my emasculation, I suffered from fits of weakness: all of which pointed in the direction of a long-stay period in a sanatorium rather than the army.

I had to sign some papers which caused me a lot of anguish. What a mess I was in!

I turned up for the medical examination which took place in an official building in Terezín, only to see a queue of young kids already waiting to be examined. There was a large glass double door, and behind it, in the next room, I saw two doctors with a nurse examining one of the youngsters, who was standing before them naked.

That was that! I turned on my heels and walked away, only to bump against Willy who had just entered the waiting room.

'What do you think you are doing?' he inquired, giving me that straight sharp look of his. I turned purple and stammered:

'I don't want to go.'

'Don't be an idiot!' He was cross now. 'You better stand here and get on with it!'

'But I am too old,' I nearly wailed.

'Nobody cares a damn how old you are. You are fifteen, remember!'

I stood there before the medical board like one condemned. Willy had stationed himself by the glass door, making sure I went through with the ordeal.

Despite all that I was still unconvinced I would ever go to England, and the thought of going neither excited nor troubled me, only the recent conscription papers remaining in the front of my mind. Some time later, unexpectedly, came the summons: I was to report at a school which was the assembly place for our transport. The flight to England was on.

Fly! That was news. Fly! They must be serious, whoever they are. The packing took three minutes. Hasty farewells, tears from Edith, hugs and send-offs, with little inner reaction on my part. But some excitement began to stir within me, some vague feeling that going was better than staying. I was tired of listening to Edith's endless remonstrations, about false friends of my father's, how naively trustful he had been, and what criminals they turned out to be.

'And look where it got you all! Your parents and brother dead, and you left with nothing but what you stand in!' Nobody would dare to do this to her, she would soon see to it. The added problem I had with all this was that she was absolutely right. She stated the situation with utmost precision. The trouble was there was nothing I could do about it.

There were three hundred young Poles and Germans to fly out to start a new life in England. But the departure was suddenly cancelled and I returned to the flat rather crestfallen and somewhat cynical. 'Of course it isn't true. This thing won't come off,' I thought to myself. 'And as to Czech pilots returning from England and our lot flying out on British planes, well, that is too fantastic to believe!'

But a week later the same order came through again. This time transport was laid on to the airfield and the three hundred of us filed across the green turf to the waiting ten Lancaster bomber planes. On the grass, in front of the machines, sat the British pilots, calmly eating their snow-white sandwiches while looking us over to see what kind of load they were taking on board for their return trip home.

I believed it now! And I made it my business to be in the front of my lot of thirty to secure as good a place as I could get, just behind the two pilots, right next to the navigator whom I watched throughout the trip working over his map, standing up and holding on to the upright bar, all the way from Prague to Carlisle, with a stop in Holland for refuelling.

I flew away from the horrors of the past, just as I was to fly away, in my frequent nightmares, from pursuers bent on killing me. But now my heart beat faster. Now I felt an excitement and anticipation, a sense of adventure gripping my dulled mind as though it was trying to shake itself out of its stupor. It felt right to be going, although I did not have the faintest notion who was behind this exodus, where we would be taken, nor what we would be doing when we arrived.

Trusting myself entirely to this venture I began to look forward to what life might have in store for me, and I felt certain that whatever happened could not possibly be worse than what I had been through.

High up in the air, enveloped by the roar of the four powerful engines, a new commitment to life began to emerge, like a tender and brittle shoot still hidden under the debris of last season's decaying growth, but strong enough to keep growing. Little did I foresee how many trying and difficult years it would take for it to emerge, develop, begin to embrace the freedom which the recent past had almost vanquished, and how the mind, lately fused and disconnected, would begin anew to be stirred by the search for meaning lost during the fierce battle for survival.

London

MY TWENTY-ONE years of life, culminating with my return to Prague from the concentration camps, when considered and compared with the forty-seven years lived in England, assume a quality of vividness, of connectedness, of integration, which the latter years fail to evoke. To face myself as I was then – the day I stepped on English soil and approached the long line of trestle tables covered in white table cloths laden with sundry snacks, tomato sandwiches and jugs of delicious cold milk, attended by numerous friendly ladies urging by gesture and smile to help ourselves, there on the tarmac of Carlisle airfield – I cannot but confess that notions of homeland and the adoption thereof were far removed from my mind. For behind the surprise and pleasure of receiving a reception of this kind lay the old cunning caution, this double agent and killer of any positive response, which would haunt me for years and years to come.

How much of this inner turmoil was apparent to the devoted volunteers who came to help with the charge of three hundred young and deeply damaged children and teenagers? When the coaches taking us from the airfield arrived at the Industrial Centre on Windermere Lake a crucial stage of our lives had begun, for this was to be a truly new start. Each of us was allotted a little room in what had been during the war effort workmen's huts, containing a number of separate tiny rooms, each furnished with a bed, a chest of drawers, a miniature wardrobe, a chair, and, in my case, the luxury of a window overlooking an old forest behind the dry stone wall. Three days of quarantine, unannounced, were spent idly watching the unrelenting rains descending from low grey skies, adding a new dimension, that of melancholia, to my other feelings. I had no understanding of what was really going on, to whom I owed my subsistence, who was responsible and in charge. Yet I took no initiative whatever to find out anything except the whereabouts of my suitcase, staying put within my vagueness and discontentedness. Not just then, of course, but on innumerable future occasions as well. I perceived life as being 'outside' of me, as though I were looking through misted glass.

I remember sitting on the shore of Lake Windermere, a daily ritual, staring across the waters to the distant hills. There were no people then. I was alone. Occasionally two horses came to graze nearby. The 'scape was large, solemn, strong, unapproachable. I observed but did not belong. Not my hills to climb, my lake to swim in or boat on, not friendly horses coming close to be patted; but remembrance of family holidays in Austrian mountains, father always ahead in his plus-fours and his stick ... swimming with father and brother, proudly crossing a lake ... friendliness, communication, joy... now all severed.

I remember Henry, our long walks together, often in total silence, each in his own world of shattered fragments of a past piercing like shrapnel into the indifferent present. Henry dear, my unconscious longing for Paul you could not assuage, nor could I give you anything of what you most needed. We went out together, yet we remained apart. Our pain was our only reality, our friendship, if it can be so called at that point, merely an accident. The real connections rested in the past and were gone forever.

I remember Chava: plump and always cheerful, a young, eager and pretty volunteer, object of such intense passion on my part. None was conveyed, the fire raging within and accentuating all the dispositions mentioned earlier. I believe my heart was overflowing; I was craving to dwell in a warm and loving presence, close to a mother-sister-lover all in one, to console, support, embrace me, for me to submerge into the living waters of love to purify and heal me.

I remember 'discovering' the Steinway grand piano behind the curtains of the stage of the large Assembly Room and my immediate flight into music as a means of giving cautious vent to my pent-up feelings. Music therapy, escape into music? Some of both, as I was to discover later in my attempt to become a musician. Playing brought about moments of temporary oblivion, if not peace, besides the bonus of a certain notoriety once it became known how much time I spent working the keys. I was given a pile of music; I gained some admirers too. But my resources of ordinary communication were strictly limited and thus I failed to cross the great divide to join the world around me.

Nevertheless, I did not want to leave Windermere and somehow managed to be one of the last to be accommodated elsewhere prior to the dissolution of the camp. Before that happened I had the privilege of two visits; my uncle Stephen from Newquay, ex-foreign legion, and my cousin from London, a pre-war refugee from Austria. It made me feel that I was not alone in England, despite the fact that our ties were tenuous. The diversion did help but did not alter my condition, and I relapsed into my unhappy state soon after they left.

The next step towards rehabilitation consisted of my placement in a Jewish hostel in Manchester, from October to December of the same year. I recall clearly the damp and freezing cold and the 'pea soup' fogs during that period, permission to practice in an unheated sitting room of a well-wisher down the road, an audition with the blind pianist Harry Isaacs, playing badly except when he went out of the room (on purpose?) and I embarked on a Chopin Nocturne which he listened to behind the door and commented favourably on when he entered again. This gave me a temporary lift, but was soon demolished by my ever active inner destroyer. We – six German orphaned Grammar school boys and I – lived under the draconian regime of deprivation of adequate care, food and warmth, owing to a warden engaged in some dishonest financial manipulations and immersed in audible domestic discord. The boys, younger than I, were docile, easily subject to authority. I suppose I felt I had nothing to lose and took the bus ride to town to approach the chairwoman of the committee and others, to describe our plight. Even now I am surprised at this one positive, planned and executed step I then took to initiate change, and it stands rather isolated among the events of those early years.

And then to London where I had originally wanted to go, be it because my father had visited it on business shortly before the war, or because my cousin was living there, or was it because I attempted to barter London in exchange for my beloved Prague, now lost to me? I was placed, through the auspices of the Jewish committee, in a large ground floor room equipped to be used as a children's day nursery, complete with tiny tables and chairs neatly painted pale blue and a wash basin in a corner behind a screen. The fireplace sported a gas fire run from a penny meter, and in another corner of the room was my bed. It was a bitterly cold London winter and the few pennies I possessed were too precious to be thrown into a meter. I was issued with tokens in lieu of payment for meals obtainable at the nearby British Restaurant, the cheap haunt of so many Jewish refugees living in that part of Hampstead.

My depression deepened and reached suicidal proportions. My isolation was almost total, the occasional friendly face and caring intention seemingly too far away to reach me. I sat for hours on a little chair by the painted little low table tracing fleeting images on the shiny surface, almost insensible to the conditions around me. I was alone, 1 had nothing real to do, nothing to live for, lost in a foreign country I did not understand, in a world which could not understand me. Instead of an ordeal by fire I was experiencing the opposite: an ordeal by cold both external and internal, when motivation and desire became frozen, rigid, lifeless.

'Why, man! There was no need for any of this! Why the hell didn't you go and look up those guys in their London office and tell them some? Those folks were there just waiting to help you!'

Why indeed! I suppose because I was crushed and beaten, sick in mind if not in body, with no fight left in me. What right did I have to ask for anything, anyway? I belonged to nobody and the world was not a place I wanted to be in, for I was an unwanted useless leftover from a war which had consumed all that was best, leaving me an unworthy survivor.

Such were my feelings, only very gradually relinquished. The committee, at that time, arranged for me to practise the piano in a nearby hostel while the girl inmates were at school. I remember little of this activity except the few occasions when my practice was terminated by the return of the girls from school who, on entering, stared and giggled when they saw me. I felt humiliated.

During one of my aimless wanderings through London I happened to pass a museum. As though nudged by an invisible hand, I entered what in fact was the Victoria and Albert museum in Kensington which, just then, was staging Picasso's work painted during the war years. I was out of touch with modernism and had not heard the name of Picasso. Now I was quite bowled over; a key seemed to have turned within me and unknown doors thrown open. I stood in front of the canvases gaping incredulously at the ugly distorted features and distorted shapes, the obvious authority of the work giving me permission to spew out the horror and ugliness which had accumulated within me. As soon as I was back in my nursery I allowed an unchecked flow of my compressed feelings full vent on any scrap of paper I could get hold of. In contrast to interpretative music making, such as I tried to engage in, with its immense restrictiveness owing to the relentless demands of style and presentation, the blank piece of paper offers an almost unlimited freedom of expression, especially when a Picasso in iconoclastic abandon throws all classical restraint to the winds. This is the point where therapy, I believe, enters.

Changes in my life-style began to take place. The nursery was deemed unsuitable for me and arrangements were made for a move, eventually to Primrose Gardens not far away, to the flat of Marion Robey, a large and friendly spinster schoolmistress who loved refugees and already had a German lodger ensconced in her basement room. The change of situation and informal domesticity and the unmistakable sense of acceptance acted like balm on my wounded self, though I could convey none of this back to my benefactress, simply because I was not sufficiently aware of the change nor had any means to communicate my feelings. Into this new haven an old upright piano was delivered through the auspices of the committee, which proved to be a complete disaster. Hardly any of the yellowed keys worked and the whole thing smelled of damp and disuse. This provoked a response on my part and I began my own search through the large stores in the West End to find an instrument, despite the fact I had no money to buy it with!

It so happened I did find an instrument I fell in love with, in a sale, for £100, quite a fortune in those days. And it also transpired when I came to mention it to my cousin that two diamond rings of my mother's had been brought by my father to her for safe keeping. They were pawned and the piano bought. Now I could embark on my playing with a will, or so I had imagined. Until now I knew nothing about the elderly French lady living on the floor above me who apparently did not share my enthusiasm, nor was able properly to appreciate the frequently violent cascades of sound, and made her own feelings felt by repeatedly knocking her broom handle against her wooden floor. That was a blow in more than one sense, my already inhibited self being made more self-conscious and deflated.

Another arrangement was made at about that time for Jewish teenagers to meet in a discussion group. Thus, one day, I found myself in a large room filled with boys and girls somewhat younger than myself sitting in a circle and discussing I know not what. The intention may have been to start a club, but my attendances soon petered out. What stands out forcibly, as well as revealingly, was my response to one particular girl I saw as being perfectly beautiful, whose closer acquaintance I would have wished for more than anything. But as soon as I became aware of my feelings I did my utmost to deny them by entirely ignoring her, neither speaking to nor even looking at her. Strangely, or perhaps not surprisingly, this deviousness resulted in generating a definite interest in me on her part, so that, before long, we established a very short-lived friendship, terminated even before her departure to the States. The initiative had been hers, my response non-committal and negative to the point of being unnecessarily, and without provocation, hurtful. In short, on meeting beauty I could not help but search out its reverse and find perverse satisfaction in being destructive.

As it appeared that music played a prominent part in my life the committee felt that full-time training in music would be in my interest and should be undertaken as soon as possible. Soon after arriving in London, while still living in my nursery, I was given an interview with a lady professor at the Guildhall School of Music. My perception of the meaning of the interview was vague, my knowledge of the Underground system incomplete, and it was very cold indeed. Oh yes, and my English was barely coherent. Therefore I arrived late, having taken the wrong train; could not explain why, causing irritation and unfriendly comment upon entering; and my hands were ice cold. I was asked to sit down and play. I have forgotten what exactly took place, I know I walked away dismayed. On another occasion, some months later in the summer, I chanced to pass the London College of Music, mistaking it for the Royal Academy I was scheduled to enter, provided I passed an audition. The college principal received me with much friendliness and chatted with me cheerfully before asking me to play. I gave as good an account of myself as I was then able to and was accepted then and there. I informed my people immediately. 'Well done, Otto, but unfortunately you went to the wrong place.' When the time arrived to attend an audition at the right place, I came on time and my hands were comfortably warm. I see in my mind's eye a large, dark and gaunt room, three tall and gaunt gentlemen standing solemnly and silently, a gesture by one for me to proceed to the instrument to play. A piece I had known all my musical life fell apart after the first half dozen bars, and I was physically and mentally incapable of starting again to repair the damage.

Despite these setbacks the period of more serious music study now began, helped by receiving regular instrumental and theoretical instruction. My daily lengthy pilgrimage by Underground to the East End of London, a place called Toynbee Hall, which I still recall with some affection, became a routine affair, as I had been given permission to practise on a respectable Bechstein upright for as many hours as I had strength to play. I say strength, not concentration: that would evaporate in about thirty to forty-five minutes: after that it degenerated into musical time structuring or a kind of occupational therapy. There certainly was a determination to keep going at all cost, yet uneasiness about the inadequate progress I was making. I occasionally took a lunch break, cash permitting; then I would indulge in sausage, mashed potatoes and mushy peas in a tiny canteen down the road. I would return to struggle on, but in a state of exhaustion, and on the return journey to Belsize Park, in the middle of the afternoon, doze off repeatedly, and jerking back painfully to wakefulness.

For evening meals I used to go to my cousin's place in Kilburn. Her solicitous care helped me to stabilise my inner emotional turmoil to some extent, but did not generate any sense of self-worth, orientation or purpose. I can now imagine what a dull and morose companion I must have been, inturned, taciturn, moody, most times on the defensive, ready for negative or destructive comment.

In today's enlightened world of psychological support and counselling it is hard to believe that my embattled soul was left to stew in its own poisoned juices. Yet I did feel a vague yearning for supportive understanding and friendship during those crucial years, someone available to me to whom I was not bound emotionally; indeed, I plucked up courage to look up two of the helpers who had been in charge of the camp in Windermere, both psychologists. One, after a friendly handshake and invitation to sit down, gave me one long look and asked: 'And how is your sex life, Otto?' He, a virile male with flaming red hair; I, a sallow youngster with pimples. He, a Freudian; I, a traumatised depressive. The channels of communication were immediately blocked, the interview lasting only a few minutes. The other professional, a middle-aged lady one would want to describe as intellectual, followed a subtler policy of discretion on the three occasions we met over a period of about three years. The last occasion was decisive, however. I had relaxed enough by then to let out some of my disturbed inner feelings, not directly, but by way of determined notions and opinions. 'You know, Otto, you are a snob!' The rejection I felt cut deep and the wound would not heal for years. I was a snob, I probably still am, but the treatment I needed lay in acceptance, not confrontation. In this context it is perhaps appropriate to mention my own professor's advice to me and the committee some time later, during my studies at the music college, to the effect that I should consult a psychiatrist for help. A psychiatrist! One who deals with mad people! I was outraged by the implication that I was not normal, since the one thing I had never been in doubt about was that I was perfectly sane, even if not 'ordinary', and I could never have admitted that I was in need of help of this kind. I, who felt the world out there to be wrong and abnormal, had no insight whatever of the extent of the damage recent events had caused, nor any awareness of how it influenced my present, grossly distorted as it was by my flounderings, vagaries and constant inner conflicts.

In 1947 I at last succeeded, with the help of my landlady and friend Marion, in securing a place at the Guildhall School of Music and thus was, inevitably, brought into closer contact with young people, many of whom came from the Services after demobilisation and therefore nearer my age. It was a turning point in my life as a fairer wind was blowing to help me on my course. Painful shyness and language difficulties added to my other problems to make the journey that much harder, but somehow I managed to hold my own and even gained a lifelong friend in John with whom I spent as much time as our studies allowed.

I know now that a great deal of work was done by him to help me achieve a measure of self-hood and orientation, preventing me from sinking into lethargy and despair. It helped to be engaged in a mildly competitive relationship, both in our music making and in our hiking exploits, whether on the South Downs or in the remote wilderness of the Scottish Highlands. The healing that took place then, unbeknown to me, must have been far-reaching.

Alongside my studies my life gradually became enriched, and often confused by new and expanding relationships and novel experiences. There were persisting elements of drift and chance as contrary dispositions met with opportunities apparently sent to me. My strong ideals now would send me to the highest peaks, my lower nature now sink me to rock bottom. But I kept coming up again, with more confidence if not greater wisdom. A thread was spun all the same, throughout this time, which I can only describe as a will to meaning which my deeper nature was desirous to unravel, and leading to a kind of inner conversion which I now see as a turning away from darkness towards light.